THE CULTURAL HERITAGE OF CHILTERN WOODS

An illustrated guide to archaeological features

ISBN 978-0-9535773-1-6
EAN 9780953577316

April 2009

Photographs by John K. Morris, unless indicated.

Published and copyright John K. Morris, The Chiltern Woodlands Project, The Lodge 90 Station Road, Chinnor, Oxon OX39 4HA Tel 01844 355503

Registered charity no 1002512
Registered in England as company no 2357329

Photos, front cover main image:
A woodland enclosure bank and ditch

Below, left to right:
Bricked up oak at Gerrards Cross
Sawpit in Pigotts Wood
Old pump at Little Hampden

Back cover:
Old beech pollards, Frithsden Beeches, Ashridge.

Chiltern Woodlands Project

John Morris works as Director of the Chiltern Woodlands Project Ltd, a registered charity formed by the Chiltern Woodlands Project Chiltern Society in 1988 with support from local councils and the Countryside Commission.

Its aims are to promote and encourage the sustainable management of woods in the Chilterns, and to increase awareness, understanding and enjoyment of Chiltern woods. The charity organises events, conferences, training days and woodland visits.

John is carrying out research into woodland history and archaeology in the Chilterns. He produced a booklet "History in Chiltern Woods – A guide to the Identification and Management of Woodland Archaeological Features" in 1999. This followed up a training session held in Pigotts Wood with Dr Nicola Bannister in 1998. These training days have been repeated annually, along with talks and other woodland visits and remain popular.

John leading a visit at Marlow Common

BBC filming at Pigotts Wood: photo Nick Wheeler Robinson

Chilterns AONB & Conservation Board

The Chilterns Area of Outstanding Natural Beauty (AONB) was designated in 1965 in recognition of the countryside being amongst the finest in England and Wales, and is a protected landscape.

The Chilterns Conservation Board was established by Parliamentary Order in  2004. It has two statutory purposes:

a. to conserve and enhance the natural beauty of the AONB; and
b. to increase the understanding and enjoyment of the special qualities of the AONB.

The Chilterns Conservation Board and Chiltern Woodlands Project have an accord and have identified their shared priorities as:
- Securing an attractive and sustainable landscape.
- Protection of existing woodlands.
- Promoting the long term sustainable management of woodlands.
- Promoting public enjoyment and understanding of woodlands and woodland heritage.
- Encouraging appropriate economic activity which supports the management of woodlands.
- Securing the protection of the special woodland heritage of woodlands.

The Chilterns Conservation Board provides the Chiltern Woodlands Project with office accommodation and in return the Project offers the Board expertise and assistance with tree and woodland work.

The research for this book was in part funded by the Chilterns AONB Woodland Research Programme, supported by the Forestry Commission and Countryside Agency (now part of Natural England) from 2004-7.

The printing of this book was made possible by a grant from the Chilterns Conservation Board's Sustainable Development Fund.

Contents

Cholesbury Camp hillfort

Ancient beech, Low Scrubs

Charcoal in roots of fallen tree

Sawpit at Pigotts Wood

Barrow at Ashridge

Stacking firewood

Acknowledgements

I would like to thank the following for their help:

Steve Rodrick and the Chilterns Conservation Board for their continuing interest and support.

David Green, Bucks County Council, who carried out the Chilterns AONB Historic Landscape Characterisation and included sections on woodlands and commonland in his report

Alan Betts and Patrick McKernan of the Forestry Commission who supported the AONB Woodlands Research programme from 2004 – 7. This led to research in High Weald, Kent Downs and Surrey Hills AONB's and published as The Cultural Heritage of woodlands in the South East, and also with Dick Greenaway working in the North Wessex Downs AONB.

Leslie Hepple and Alison Doggett's book on The Chilterns is an important reference.

John Laker and other volunteers from Archaeology in Marlow – Their ROMADAM project researched two woodland iron age hillforts at Medemenham; mapped the first world war practice trenches in Pullingshill Wood, Marlow Common and examined an enclosure in Warren Wood, Marlow.

Gary Marshall, National Trust regional archaeologist who spent three years with volunteers mapping the archaeological features of Park Wood on the Bradenham estate.

Sheffield Hallam University who produced a Woodland Heritage Manual in 2008. I helped organise a couple of the workshops for this publication, including a visit to Spring Wood.

Dr Tim Southern and Susan Gibson have been looking at a number of woods in South Oxfordshire. They helped measure the bank profiles in Pigotts Wood in 2008.

Nick Wheeler Robinson for his enthusiastic support of the woodland archaeology workshops held at Pigotts.

Liz Manley and Rachel Sanderson who have been coordinating volunteer research for the Special Trees and Woods of the Chilterns project (a project run by the Chilterns Woodlands Project, thanks to support from the Heritage Lottery Fund) and the volunteers for their records.

Thanks also to Glyn Kuhn for his patient help with the design and layout for this book, and to my wife Joanna for her support, for reading the draft and making helpful suggestions.

Aim of this book

The aim of this book is to illustrate and try to explain the various bumps and hollows and other earthworks that add such character to Chiltern woods. I hope this will raise awareness of their importance as these features are a part of our heritage and can help us to understand the past.

It should help woodland owners, managers, advisors and others to understand some of the archaeological features found in woods in the Chilterns. As a result they should be able to protect them from potentially damaging operations when carrying out woodland management.

The remains from earlier land uses have been weathered and eroded over the years, and may have been buried in places, but can still reveal interesting information about the history of the area. Many features survive in a much better condition in woods than in the surrounding countryside, where ploughing or development has taken place.

The South East is the most wooded region of England with some 40% of its ancient woods. It is not clear what woodland archaeology there is, as so little is scheduled or surveyed. Woodlands have been the black hole of archaeology and have been overlooked by many archaeologists who often identify likely sites by aerial photography, which the trees hide. You really have to visit the wood at the right time of year to see them. Features in woods still exist, as both major and minor earthworks, rather than as buried features in a ploughed or developed landscape.

National Parks and AONB's in England

Introduction

A lot has happened in the ten years since I wrote History in Chiltern Woods. Interest in the ancient woods has increased. The courses I have been running at Pigotts Wood since 1988 have continued every year since, with the numbers of participants increasing each year. I have also given numerous talks and led guided walks on this subject. I presented papers on woodland features at two well attended Chilterns Historic Environment Conferences, held in 2003 and 2008. I carried out research into woodland features as part of the AONB's woodland research programme funded by the Forestry Commission and English Nature from 2004 – 7.

The Chiltern Woodlands Project has been running its very successful Special Trees and Woods project since January 2006, thanks to Heritage Lottery funding and support from the Chilterns Conservation Board. About 50 volunteers have been researching and recording the stories behind the trees and woods of the Chilterns. The results are in the "Special" section of the Chilternsaonb website. This website also has a "woodland web" section with more information about the history of the woods.

We were fortunate to have Dr Oliver Rackham as our guest speaker at our 2008 conference, as his books have inspired many of us to research our ancient woods. He states, in an article for our News of the Woods newsletter in 2008, that the Chilterns have been the second biggest concentration of natural woodland in England for over a thousand years. Unlike many lesser wooded areas they have changed greatly. In wood pastures the trees, often beech, were scattered in grassland. They were usually pollarded, cut like coppice stools but 2 – 3 metres above the ground so that cattle, sheep and deer could not eat the young shoots. Chiltern woods had the job of supplying firewood to the growing city of London. In the eighteenth century this declined through increasing competition from coal. It was replaced by the demands of the High Wycombe furniture industry.

Woodlands are an important part of the historical landscape of the Chilterns with many cultural associations. The archaeological evidence that survives in the woods can help explain the development of woodland management in this area.

The Chilterns AONB has about 10,000 hectares (ha) of ancient woodland, (excluding woods under 2ha which may also be ancient with features of historical interest). Many ancient woods are now known to contain features of the historic environment, including the old trees themselves. Nearly 80% of the woods in the Chilterns, some 13,300 ha, are privately owned, with ownership ranging from less than one hectare to over 400 ha.

Ancient Woods are now seen as an integral part of England's historic landscapes and many contain a wealth of features unaltered by cultivation and disturbance. Woods have often protected archaeological features where they have not survived in the farmed countryside; but they can be damaged by modern forestry equipment and harvesting practices if care is not taken to identify and consider them.

I produced a report on a Pilot Ancient Woodland Survey in the Chilterns that I carried out in 2007. This pilot study found an increase in ancient woodland cover in 20 randomly selected 1km survey squares from 11.7% shown in the published ancient woodland inventory available on websites such as www.magic.gov.uk to 14.2%. This is similar to the increase found in more detailed studies in other parts of the South East. The proportion of ancient semi-natural woods was found to be 53% greater and the amount of plantation on ancient woodland sites 19% less than shown in the Chilterns inventory maps available on websites. The reason may in part be due to over simplification of woodland types in the original inventory by the Nature Conservancy Council, which was more concerned about identifying the best ancient woods for their flora rather than for other features.

Prehistoric & Historic Period Table for England

	Dates (approximate)	
	From	To
NEOLITHIC (STONE AGE)	4,000 BC	2,500BC
BRONZE AGE	2,500 BC	750BC
IRON AGE	750 BC	AD 43
ROMAN	AD 43	AD 410
ANGLO SAXON	410	1066
MEDIEVAL	1066	1540
POST MEDIEVAL	1540	Present

(from Bannister N.R. Woodland Archaeology in Surrey)

Recent Policies

The importance of the historic environment and cultural heritage of ancient woodlands has increased considerably over the last ten years. It is a key part of the government's Keepers of Time policy, launched in 2005. This recognises the importance of ancient woods and old trees for their historic and cultural values as well as for biodiversity. However the aim of restoring Plantations on Ancient Woodland Sites could cause harm to these features of ancient woods, unless they are identified and better understood. Another policy to encourage the production of wood fuel (the most traditional use of woodlands!) could also lead to damage to features if care is not taken to identify and protect them.

Planning Policy Statement 9 (2005) states that local planning authorities should identify any areas of ancient woodland in their areas that do not have statutory protection (eg as an SSSI). Ancient woodland is a valuable biodiversity resource. Once lost it cannot be recreated.

It is also a theme within the Strategy for England's Trees, Woods and Forests published by defra in the summer of 2007. This has been followed up by an Action Plan 2008 -12 in 2008. One of the objectives is to enhance the contribution of trees, woods and forests to wider landscapes, and ensure their historic and cultural values are being protected and appreciated. Another is to conserve ancient woods and veteran trees, ensure they are resilient to climate change and provide opportunities for people to enjoy woodland wildlife

More locally the Management Plan for the Chilterns Area of Outstanding Natural Beauty 2008-13 produced by the Chilterns Conservation Board recognises the role of its rich historic environment in shaping this nationally important landscape.

UK Woodland management standards

"Woodland management should conserve biodiversity and safeguard and enhance landscape and heritage resources." (UK Forestry Accord 1996 - in UK Forestry Standard 1998). Scheduled monuments and other important archaeological sites, historic and cultural features should be protected. Our links with and understanding of the past, and our appreciation of the present are thereby maintained. Protecting historic features will also often help maintain the ecological interest and landscape importance of the wood.

Consultation and funding

The Forestry Commission's Woodland Officers will visit woods to examine proposals for work under a Felling Licence or England Woodland Grant Scheme application when felling or new planting is considered. Work proposals are then published on a public register during the consultation process. The applicant or agent should indicate any designated sites on the application forms and accompanying maps. Funding may sometimes be available for archaeological and ecological survey under the Assessment Grants if the Forestry Commission considers it necessary. Grants to help restore Plantations on Ancient Woodland Sites in the Chilterns may be available; as is funding for long term woodland management plans.

Natural England also has a role in woodland management as one of the options under Higher Level Stewardship. They too should take account of historic features found in ancient woodland.

Funding is also available in the Chilterns under the LEADER programme to support farmers and foresters invest in capital expenditure.

The Cultural Heritage of Woodlands in the Chilterns

The Chiltern Hills form a unique landscape, different in character from the other chalk or woodland regions of England. The Chilterns were designated by the government as an Area of Outstanding Natural Beauty in 1965 and are nationally important. 800 km2 was then designated and the area increased to 833km2 following a boundary review in 1990. However the AONB boundary is drawn around major towns and villages, so places like High Wycombe and Chesham, which were centres for the furniture and woodworking industries, are outside the AONB boundary. The Chilterns are on London's doorstep, and immediately adjacent to several large towns which have influenced the management of the woods since medieval times. The woods were a valuable resource and at times were more important than the neighbouring agricultural land.

The Chiltern Hills form a distinct "Natural Area" characterised by its beech woods. The beech/yew woods on the chalk are of international importance, with rare plants associations. Yew is now under-represented in this type of woodland in the Chilterns. Beech woods with bluebells are also a major landuse on the clay with flint covered dip slope. Beech high forest has been important in parts of the Chilterns for at least the last 400 years, but other types of beech wood also exist and perhaps were more common in the past.

The Chilterns are separated from the North Wessex Downs AONB by the River Thames. The ridge of hills with its scarp facing north west over the Vale of Aylesbury runs across four counties, Oxfordshire, Buckinghamshire, Hertfordshire and Bedfordshire. The first two counties are in the South East England Government region the others in Eastern England. The AONB is split in two by Luton as the boundary was drawn to exclude towns.

The Chilterns AONB and Chilterns 'Natural Area'

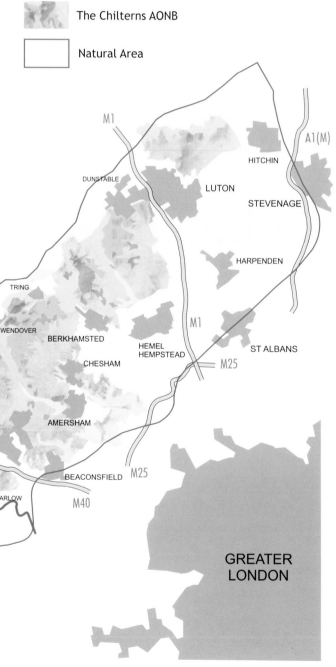

The Chilterns AONB

Natural Area

Topography, Geology and Soils

The Chiltern Hills are formed by a southwest to northeast aligned ridge of chalk (from the cretaceous period 65 to 95 million years ago). The overall topographical character of the Chilterns has been classified into four broad regions; Scarp and Foothills, Plateau and Dipslope, the Arterial Valleys and the Thames Fringes (Chilterns Conservation Board 2001). Ancient woods are mainly found on the hilltops of the plateau and dipslope, where the chalk is overlain by extensive deposits of glacial "clay with flints" and other "drift" deposits of sands and gravels laid down during the Anglian glaciation around 400,000 years ago. These form heavy, acidic, stony brown earths which are difficult to cultivate and lack fertility.

At its highest point, in Wendover Woods, it reaches over 900 feet (272 metres). It is dissected by a number of chalk streams that run down to the Rivers Thames and Colne. Modern transport routes follow many of these valleys through the Chilterns, as does the Grand Union canal and a number of rail lines into London.

The Chilterns is recognised as an area of ancient countryside with small farms, numerous ancient woods, early clearances and enclosures and dispersed settlement. This contrasts with the planned open field landscape of Aylesbury Vale seen from the Chilterns scarp, which for the most part lacks ancient woodland.

The Chilterns AONB is rich in ancient woodland, with an estimated 14% of its area covered by this special habitat compared to the average for England as a whole of 3%. The hilltops are densely wooded and have been for many hundreds of years. At the time of the Domesday survey in 1086 AD the Chilterns are thought to have had a woodland cover of well over one third of the area. It now has a total woodland cover of over 21%, with over 18,000 ha of woodland, making it one of the more wooded parts of the country. England has on average just 9% woodland.

Ancient woods contain many features of historical and archaeological interest. Without care, these features which help give the area its character, and each wood its "sense of place", could easily be damaged and perhaps lost for good. It is not possible to recreate these features in any meaningful way if they are accidentally harmed. Restoration may depend on the

Wooded hilltops north of High Wycombe

degree of damage. However the intention is not to freeze the landscape at one point in time, but to raise awareness of the significance of the past land-use while considering its future. The woods form an intimate mosaic with both arable and grasslands.

The figures (right) are from the Ancient Woodland Inventory (Forestry Commission version 2003) and are for woods over 2ha. It is estimated that a further 690 ha of woods exist that are smaller than the 2ha cut off point used in the national inventory of woodlands. These small woods have not yet been identified as ancient or not.

Chilterns AONB total area	**83,828**	hectares
All woodland area	**17,588**	hectares
% of AONB woodland cover	**21%**	
Ancient woodland area	**9,830**	hectares
Ancient Semi-Natural Woodland	**5,754**	hectares
% of ancient woodland	**59%**	
Plantation on Ancient Woodland Sites	**4,076**	hectares
% of ancient woodland	**41%**	

Chilterns AONB with all woods
(Forestry Commission woods shown darker green)

Woodlands in the 21st Century

Many woodlands, especially smaller woodlands, are under managed, even neglected. Management has been affected by long term decline of timber prices, notably for beech, which has depressed the market and led to less activity. The climate is changing and becoming less predictable, and the ageing stands of beech will result in long term changes in the woodland landscape as these trees are replaced by ash and other trees. The promotion of wood as a renewable fuel may stimulate management. However many woods are now more valuable as places for recreation and as landscape features than for their timber.

A quality beech - many of the best beech have been felled for timber

Woodland History of the Chilterns

The woodland area in the Chilterns has not remained constant but has fluctuated with the demand for agricultural or woodland produce and under the influence of human population pressures. Land that may once have been farmed was sometimes abandoned and "tumbled down" through scrub to become woodland. In other cases it may have been cleared and later replanted. Many larger woods had fields cut out of them in medieval times. This process was known as assarting. Some fields remained open whilst others later grew back into woodland.

There is evidence to indicate that parts of the Chilterns must have been cleared of woodland by the Iron Age, as there are numerous hillforts, enclosures and features such as Grims Ditch, that seem likely to have been constructed in a more open landscape. However it would appear that it became more heavily wooded in the Dark Ages following the Roman period. Surprisingly little is known of this period as it has had limited investigation.

There is some evidence of earlier field systems becoming colonised with woodland possibly as a result of a reduction in population: the same thing may have happened after the Black Death in the 14th century.

Although most of the area was not a Royal hunting forest, it is clear that the area east of the Norman castle in Berkhamsted in Hertfordshire was used for hunting deer by the Black Prince, amongst others. Parts of South Oxfordshire north of Reading may have been a hunting forest but this did not last long.

The management of the woodlands has been heavily influenced by their proximity to London. The River Thames was navigable in the medieval period downstream from places such as Henley and Marlow, which developed as riverside ports. Fashions have also played a part, with some landowners clearing woodland for agriculture and others planting trees and woods for a variety of reasons.

Berkhamsted Castle

Designed landscapes

In parts of Buckinghamshire and Hertfordshire hornbeam woods occur. Hornbeam and beech were also used for hedging around woods. Wild cherry and ash are frequently found on the edges of beechwoods on the clay with flints.

Whitebeam, field maple, wych elm and hazel are trees found along with a range of shrubs such as wayfaring tree, guelder rose and spindle on the chalky soils. Oak, birch, rowan and aspen may be found on the more acid sands and gravels of the plateau. Holly is found in many plateau beechwoods.

Designed landscapes, such as parks, are a feature of the Chilterns and these changed with the fashion and the great designers of the day, including Charles Bridgeman in the 1720s and Lancelot "Capability" Brown in the 1760s for example at Ashridge. Humphrey Repton was involved in landscaping the Shardeloes Estate near Amersham, Bucks.

Woods were cleared in some places during the 18th and 19th centuries when farming prices encouraged owners to do so, yet at the same time a neighbouring owner might plant new mixed plantations, with introduced conifers, perhaps with shooting interest in mind.

Chiltern woods were often more valuable than the surrounding agricultural land but this fluctuated. In Anthony Mansfield's MSc thesis (from 1952) on the history of the management of Chiltern beechwoods, he quotes that:
 "52 acres of Upper Wood at Shirburn, which had been worth 7 shillings per acre per annum, were cleared in 1747 for agriculture (Portebello Farm) and then rented out for 10 shillings an acre."

Well managed beechwoods at the end of the 19th century were returning five or six times the annual income of the adjoining land. Daniel Witney, President of the Surveyors' Institute, wrote in a court case 1890/91 involving the West Wycombe estate that the woodland returned 30 shillings per acre, but if the land was cleared and cultivated he doubted it would return more than 5 shillings per acre.

The maximum value attained by beechwoods was reached in 1875; the price fell sharply between 1900 and 1914 when timber imports had a big impact.

West Wycombe House

The Bodgers

In the Chilterns there was a tradition, which lasted over 250 years, in which skilled woodsmen turned chairlegs, spindles and other products on simple but effective pole lathes out in the woods. At the start of the eighteenth century this was a cottage industry. By the nineteenth century Windsor chairs were being assembled from the turned parts made by the bodgers, to the seats (known as bottoms) in numerous factories in and around High Wycombe. The town soon became the furniture centre for the country and the chairs were sent to all parts, with many being exported.

The production of other turnery wares was important in the town of Chesham in 1801 using local beech, and by 1910 it was a centre of brush making. Checkendon in South Oxfordshire also had a brush factory, using short lengths of timber, which could be cut from lower grades of beech tree.

Forestry Commission

The Forestry Commission started work in 1919 after the First World War to produce a strategic reserve of timber. Many of the woods managed by the Forestry Commission were planted with conifers, which were sometimes used as a nurse for beech and oak.

During the Second World War many woods were again heavily exploited for firewood and for timber. Some 2,300 acres were clear felled between 1939 and 1947. Many other woods had been over thinned, selectively felling the useful trees. Beech was used for tent pegs, (made by the million in Stoke Row, Oxon) rifle butts, plywood for aircraft and for fuel. Despite this exploitation most of the woods have regenerated and survived but in some cases they were replanted with conifers.

A team of woodland workers c1880 - copyright Wycombe Musuem

Forestry Commission Inventory of Private Woods in Chilterns 1947 - 1949

(woods over 5 acres, approximately 2 hectares) from Anthony Mansfield thesis in 1952. It is not clear how much of the Chilterns he covered in this study, figures are probably only for Bucks & Oxon.

Type	Acres	Hectares	% of Private Woods
High Forest			
Conifer	1,408	569	4.5
Mixed	1,249	505	4.0
Broadleaved	22,290	9,020	70.2
Total	**24,947**	**10,096**	**78.5**
Coppice with Standards	479	194	1.5
Coppice only	351	142	1.0
Total	**830**	**336**	**2.5**
Scrub	**1,737**	**703**	**5.5**
Devastated	**1,605**	**650**	**5.0**
Felled before August 1939	249	100	0.5
Felled after August 1939	2,315	937	7.5
Total	**2,564**	**1,307**	**8.0**
Grand Total	**31,683**	**12,822**	

Plus 832 acres (336 ha) that were owned by the Forestry Commission at this time. Beech was the main tree found on 20,172 acres (8,163 ha) and larch was the main conifer on 1236 acres (500ha) in private woods in 1947.

The 1997 Forestry Commission census shows the commonest trees in the Chilterns were

6,090 ha beech
2,242 ha ash
1,798 ha oak
910 ha birch

Conifers cover 3,447 ha, about 21% of the woods, with larch 1,330 ha being twice as common as pines 623ha, Douglas fir 558ha and Norway spruce 466ha.

Ancient Beechwoods

The ancient beechwoods of the Chilterns occur in a variety of forms and most were not plantations, although some have certainly since been replanted. They included beech pollards, in old wood-pasture, on the formerly extensive commons and common woods. Beech fuel was cut in coppices, formerly known as "hillwork", where wood was cut for fuel by people from parishes that extended up the scarp from the vale. Historically some parishes had detached areas up in the Chilterns to provide a resource at a distance from the main settlements. Other parishes were very narrow to give access to the River Thames in Oxfordshire and connections between the hill and the vale in both Buckinghamshire and Oxfordshire.

Map of Oxfordshire parishes in 19th century and woodland cover

(from Chilterns Historic Landscape Characterisation Study)

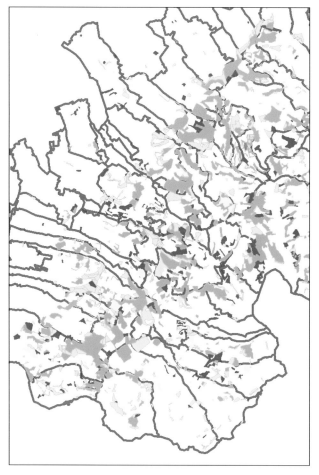

Map shows narrow parish strips running down to the River Thames.

Former beech coppice

Beech high forest is where individual tall trees grow, mixed with species such as ash and oak, and managed on a selection system of thinning.

The draft Victoria County History for Oxfordshire (available on a website) reports a survey of 1388 that suggests the main woodland products were firewood and other small wood, like the 'crop' of Bixbrand wood, which was reserved to the lord. It may be that large areas of wood were not very systematically managed at that time, however: 55 acres wood in Bix Gibwyn and 100 acres in Bixbrand was worth nothing because there was no underwood! I believe this is an indication that the wood may well have been composed of large shade bearing beech trees (similar to today?). This was 40 years after the Black Death, which may have reduced the local population.

In Hepple & Doggett's book "The Chilterns" they report that in 1598 at Lewknor, it is said that "they do not fell all the wood together but glean and draw out that which is about the growth of 21 years" (I think this could be a reference to selective felling or thinning rather than coppicing?).

The Black Prince, who owned Berkhamsted Castle in 1358, is reported as giving gifts of beech trees but having to buy in oak timber. In 1612, at Berkhamsted Frith a valuation recorded 1,214 acres and contained over 25,000 beeches, 1,500 oaks and 212 ash trees. There were riots here when various attempts were made to enclose the land and remove the commoners rights.

Beech regeneration in Common Wood

The following quotes from **www.visionofbritain.org.uk/travellers** also show that beech was the dominant tree in many Chiltern woods and that the area was heavily wooded.

William Camden in 1607 says "Chiltern got that name according to the very nature of the soile of Chalkie marle, which the English men termed Cylt or Chilt. For all of it mounteth aloft with whitish hilles, standing upon a mixt earth of clay and chalke clad with groves and woods, wherein is much Beech, and it was altogether unpassable in times past by reason of trees." He also says in 1610 of the Hundred of Henley in South Oxfordshire, that it is "mounting high with hilles and beset with thicke woods" and that "Neere unto it, Henley upon Tamis sheweth it selfe in the verie confines of the shires. The inhabitants whereof bee for the most part watermen, who make their chiefest gaine by carrying downe in their barges wood and corne to London".

Daniel Defoe writing in 1727 says "Vast quantity of beech wood, which grows in the woods of Buckinghamshire more plentifully than in any other part of England. This is the most useful wood, for some uses, that grows, and without which, the city of London would be put to more difficulty …. Beech quarters for divers uses, particularly chairmakers, and turnery wares. The quantity of this, brought from hence, is almost incredible, and yet so is the country overgrown with beech in those parts, that it is bought very reasonable, nor is there like to be any scarcity of it for time to come. "

William Cobbett's diary for June 24, 1822 states "After Chesham, I passed through a wood. Here there are only two sorts of trees, beech and oak: but … none of that stuff which we generally call underwood: the trees standing very thick in some places: the shade so complete as never to permit herbage below: no bushes of any sort; and nothing to impede your steps but little spindling trees here and there grown up from the seed. The trees here are as lofty, too. The oaks seem here to vie with the beeches in size as well as in loftiness and straightness. I saw several oaks which I think were more than eighty feet high, and several with a clear stem of more than forty feet."

A classic Chilterns bluebell wood

Woodland Archaeology

This is the study of the historical features and remains that often survive as earthworks in woods. There are two types, those that relate to earlier phases of woodland management, including long lived trees themselves, and those features that now happen to be found in woodland.

Woods are normally a stable part of the countryside and often protect features that have been lost through ploughing of agricultural land or through housing and other development.

Past woodland management features include banks, sawpits, charcoal hearths and the trees themselves as coppice stools, stubs and pollards.

Of particular interest locally are industrial activities such as the clay industries, charcoal burning, bodging, iron-smelting and timber production.

Woodland features cannot normally be seen by aerial survey, you need to visit the woods! This is best done in late winter when vegetation has died down. Young spring growth can show up some features. Earthworks can be harder to find in summer due to the shade of trees and development of vegetation. In autumn leaf fall can bury many subtle features.

Both tree roots and forestry operations can harm archaeological features so care is needed to take account of the historic environment when planting or planning management tasks.

Commons

Some commons were once very large. The area known as Wycombe Heath, between High Wycombe and Amersham in Buckinghamshire, was shared by seven parishes and may have originally been a Saxon chase, used for hunting. The former extent of commonland and manorial "waste" in the Chilterns has been greatly reduced by enclosure; however over 2,000 hectares remain. Most of these commons used to be grazed but since this ceased many have developed into scrub and secondary woodland, but in some cases old open grown trees survive. Many of the commons were managed as wood pasture, with grazing animals kept beneath an open canopy of pollarded trees. There are also several common woods where the community had access to them for resources; some of these may have been enclosed later and taken into private management.

Most commons are privately owned although rights of common have their origin in local custom which date back to the medieval period and possibly earlier. These commoners rights are attached to particular properties and include, for example, the right to graze stock, to enable pigs to forage on beechmast and acorns (pannage), to remove peat for the hearth (turbary), to fish (piscary) and to collect bracken or firewood (estovers).

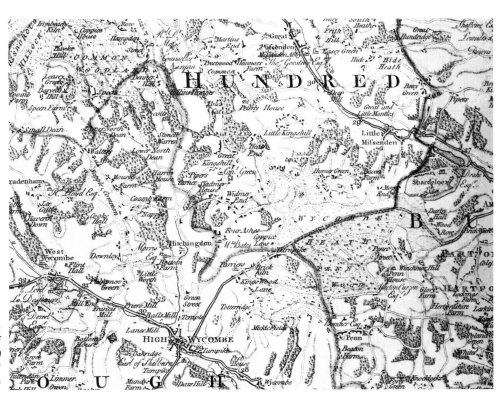

Map of Wycombe Heath from Jeffreys Map of Bucks 1770 (Bucks Archaeological Society)

Commons performed an important economic role in the Chilterns as places for grazing livestock and as a crucial source of fuel.

The location of commons and the activities upon them are due in part to their physical characteristics, many are typically found on the least fertile soils. Topography also seems to be a determining factor as the majority of commons are found beyond the scarp and are orientated in a northwest to south east alignment. 85% of commons within the AONB are located on the spurs, typically above 150m.

Some commons were also important for communications and used as drove routes to move animals to market.

R. Davis in 1794 in the Hampden Estate record says "The succession of young trees in beechwoods is much injured by admitting sheep and cattle into them – some improvement might be made in keeping better fences, particularly against commons where a wide ditch is an essential part of the mound".

Ponds are frequently found on former open commons where they used to provide water for grazing livestock. The layers of sediment may contain pollen grains and other evidence that helps interpret the past environment. Over time deposits build up in layers in the pond, which can be dated. The exact point in these layers that any historic artefact or historic pollen evidence is found is critical to this dating.

Parliamentary Enclosure of Commons

The main reason for the disappearance of commons and heathland was the advance in agricultural technology, which made possible and profitable the cultivation of land hitherto regarded as waste. This led to the introduction in the 19th century of Parliamentary Enclosure Acts known as the General Acts of 1845 which enabled common land to be enclosed for 'improvement' for agriculture and for profit; commons such as Wycombe, Holmer Heath, Penn (Bucks), Wiggington Common, (Herts) and Goring Heath (Oxon) were enclosed in this process. The commoners were often given allotments in return for forfeiting their rights to use land.

Pond on Naphill Common

The Cultural Heritage of Woodlands in the Chilterns

Pollards

On the more wooded commons, pollarding was sometimes carried out to provide fodder and firewood. Pollarding is the cutting of branches about ten feet or so up the trunk out of reach of browsing animals, which allowed new shoots to re-grow. This cutting has prolonged the life of these trees. Good examples of former wood pasture with ancient pollards survive at Burnham Beeches, Bucks; Frithsden Beeches at Ashridge, in Hertfordshire; and Naphill Common in Bucks. The Nettlebed Commons in Oxfordshire have areas of old beech coppice which were cut to fuel the local brick kiln.

The Lords of the Manor often retained the right to timber, i.e. the more valuable building material, while commoners had the rights to the branchwood for fuel.

A number of woods known as common woods still exist and these may have had a different usage in the past. Enclosure and changes in management practices over time mask the way the woods used to function.

Beech coppice at Chinnor Hill

Coppice

Coppicing is an ancient form of management where poles are cut near ground level on a rotation of 7 to 15 or more years, to provide a regular supply of material. New poles grow again from the cut stump if there is enough light and it is protected from browsing animals. This process prolongs the life of the tree and some of our oldest trees were once coppiced. There may have been more coppices in the South Oxfordshire Chilterns in the past as many woods here are known as copses. Coppiced trees, because they survive so long, may retain genetic information about their original natural distribution, rather than those introduced by planting.

Beech coppice may sometimes have been more like shredding, where some of the small side branches are stripped off a stubby trunk to provide bundles of twigs, known as faggots, for fuel.

Most formerly coppiced woods in the Chilterns have been converted to "High Forest" with tall timber trees. In most cases it is not desirable to reinstate coppicing unless the coppice structure of hazel or hornbeam is still obvious and there are good conservation or economic reasons so to do. Hornbeam coppice is mainly found in southeast Buckinghamshire and Hertfordshire.

Frithsden Beeches, Ashridge

Ancient Woods

Ancient Woods have been continuously wooded since 1600 AD (Natural England and the Forestry Commission use this definition).

These woods are defined as either Semi-Natural, composed of native species which have arisen by natural means but with their condition modified by management, or Plantations on Ancient Woodland Sites (PAWS) where conifers and other trees have been planted.

Ancient woods can be identified on the early maps of this area or from other documentary evidence going back up to 400 years. These woods often have a rich ground flora of species only found in woodland conditions, and other wildlife associated with a long continuity of woodland cover. They are of historical and ecological interest in their own right. The relationship of woodlands to the farmed landscape and the way this has changed over time is of historical importance. Much can be learnt about the area's past by studying the land-use changes that can still be identified from features in woodlands today.

English Nature produced lists of plant species that may indicate an ancient woodland *(see appendix)*; the more of these species that occur in the wood the more likely it is to be ancient. However this is also influenced by other factors such as the soil type and tree canopy. For example, more plant species may be found on chalk soils than on acid gravels, and beech woods are too shady for many species.

Wood anenomes

Ancient Semi-natural woodlands

There are at least 5,754 hectares of this woodland type in the Chilterns AONB which are considered to be of the highest nature conservation value and also of considerable cultural and historic interest. They retain features that are not found in more recent woods.

Plantations on ancient woodland sites

These woods have been restocked by planting, often with conifers, possibly as a nurse for broad-leaved timber trees. There are 4,076 hectares of this type of replanted woodland in the Chilterns shown on the inventory. However a recent pilot survey indicates that this may be an over estimate and that remnants of semi-natural woodland may survive within these sites.

The government's Keepers of Time policy published in 2005 encourages the removal of introduced conifers from these woodlands in order to restore them to native species. There are risks involved if heavy equipment is used to fell and extract this timber as many of these sites retain features of interest, but which have not been recorded.

Plantation marked for thinning next to old hornbeams

Some broadleaved trees, such as sycamore or sweet chestnut, may also indicate plantations of non native species, but these may be old and considered less of a problem than evergreen conifers.

Secondary Woods

Secondary Woods are woods that have developed on land that has been cleared for agriculture. Many areas in the Chilterns may have been more open from Bronze Age to Roman times before becoming wooded again. It is thought that the boundaries of many medieval woods in the Chilterns may have been fixed by the thirteenth century.

This term is now often used interchangeably with recent woods to indicate woods that have developed since 1600 i.e. which are not ancient.

Recent Woods

Recent Woods have developed, or been planted, since 1600AD. Landscaping on country estates through tree planting has occurred since this date. Conifer planting was popular through much of the twentieth century. Some new broadleaved woods have been planted, sometimes with help from grants from the 1980's. These "amenity" woods may have been created for landscape, sporting or economic reasons.

Other areas have become native woodland by natural regeneration of indigenous trees and shrubs. New native woods are particularly found on the commons and on areas of former chalk grassland, especially on the scarp, where livestock grazing ceased.

Woodland names can be useful in deciding the type of woodland, but be aware that names can change over time so it is important to find the earliest name possible. Woods, groves and shaws are all Saxon names, coppice and copses are from Norman French, while plantation and covert are more recent.

Grim's Ditch at Aldbury Nowers

Scheduled Monuments

The larger and more important archaeological features in woodland may have been identified and protected by law as Scheduled Monuments under the 1979 Ancient Monuments and Archaeological Areas Act. They can be found on the website www.magic.gov.uk

Examples include the Iron Age Hillforts at Cholesbury, Boddington in Wendover Woods and Pulpit Hill near Princes Risborough, (all Bucks) which are all in woods.

The Whiteleaf and Bledlow Crosses, both in Buckinghamshire, were cut in open areas on the scarp and were visible from many miles away. These chalk figures need to be kept clear of encroachment by trees and scrub from nearby woods.

View of Whiteleaf Cross

The mysterious linear feature Grim's Ditch is a massive bank and ditch, its course is in places in woodland or marked by a belt of trees. It occurs in separated stretches in Oxfordshire, Buckinghamshire and Hertfordshire. The term "Grim" is a Saxon one and was used by them to describe huge existing earthworks that they could not explain.

There are 122 Scheduled Ancient Monuments in the Chilterns AONB and 15 parks and gardens on English Heritage's register. Most of these will have a management agreement in place with English Heritage. English Heritage can be contacted about Scheduled Monuments, management grants, repair and consent for works.

Archaeological Advice

The county archaeologists are willing to advise on the management of features of concern. They have records of the many known historical and archaeological sites in their County Sites and Monuments Record. They should be consulted about designated sites and major historic features.

Archaeological features are frequently found hidden in Chiltern woods (sometimes by young trees, holly, brambles and bracken), and many have not been formally identified or protected!

County Record Offices and libraries hold collections of maps and documents which may prove useful.

Ecological Sites

National Nature Reserves, Sites of Special Scientific Interest (SSSI's) and species protected under the Wildlife and Countryside Act 1981 or CROW Act (2000) require consent for work from Natural England.

Summer vegetation may hide features such as this earthwork

Winter is the best time to see features in woods

Survey Methods

Winter visits

The main method of identifying features in woods is likely to be through walking the site. The best time of year to look for many features is in winter or early spring (from January through to May) when rank vegetation such as bracken, brambles & nettles have died down and before the trees come into leaf. In autumn, falling leaves can hide quite sizeable banks and ditches and other more subtle features. Drought, frost and snow and low angle winter light may all help to show subtle banks and hollows.

Sometimes features can be picked out by changes in vegetation. Old ditches may be damp and fertile and banks dry and stony, so different plants such as mosses or dogs mercury may grow. Disturbed soil and ground affected by fires may also result in a change in the species of plant. Mapping the flora can pick out some otherwise hidden features.

Recording / sketch mapping

Examples of recording forms are in the appendices of this book. Examples of some the sketch maps I have drawn to show the position of woodland features are also included. These are indicative maps to locate roughly where banks and pits can be found. It is a quick and easy method that works best in smaller woods when you can easily work out where you are!

Traditional mapping techniques using tapes, measuring wheels, theodolites etc may be needed in larger more complex woods such as Park Wood, Bradenham *(see case study later)*.

Surveying in Bradenham woods

New Technology

The identification of many ancient features in the landscape is often possible by using aerial photos. However this is not normally possible in woods as the trees hide any soil or crop marks. Aerial photos can be used to identify patterns in neighbouring farmland, such as old roads, field systems and hedgerows, and will show how the wood fits in the landscape. Recent aerial photographs are held by the County Council Planning Departments, others are available on websites.

Geographic Positioning Systems (GPS)

These hand held portable devices can be used to map features within woods as points (for pits) or lines on map (for example to show banks and tracks). However the accuracy can vary as trees and canopy cover can interfere with satellite signals. The system relies on lining up a number of satellites to fix a position. The signal can bounce off the canopy and trunks of trees producing a certain amount of error. Evergreen conifers can be difficult as can broadleaved tree canopy in summer. More expensive systems can be used to correct these errors.

LiDAR

A new remote aerial sensing technique using lasers known as LiDAR can be used to strip off the tree cover using a computer programme to reveal the ground surface as if the trees did not exist. This is an expensive technique that requires flights over the landscape to be studied. It will identify targets, but to interpret the results on the ground survey is likely to be needed.

Until recently woods have been a black hole for archaeologists working in offices plotting features from aerial photographs, as the tree cover has hidden major earthworks and small lumps and bumps from view. Now Forest Research (an arm of the Forestry Commission) can use LiDAR to plot features beneath the trees. LiDAR stands for 'light detection and ranging'; the technology works by "bouncing" harmless laser energy off the forest in much the same way as radar ('radio detection and ranging') bounces radio waves off solid objects. LiDAR sends laser signal pulses from an aircraft and then measures the time taken for the signals to return to the recording instruments in the aircraft. The minimum time shows the top of the tree canopy and the maximum time the ground surface (or possibly dense vegetation such as brambles) and advanced computer software can be used to analyse the responses and build up pictures of the ground. The next stage is to visit the wood on the ground to see what LiDAR has identified. It is also possible to work out the height of the trees with this equipment. The best time to fly would be in late winter or early spring before the trees come in to leaf and before ground vegetation develops, as this would give the clearest picture of any earthworks.

LiDAR computer generated, hillshaded images of Savernake Forest in Wiltshire.

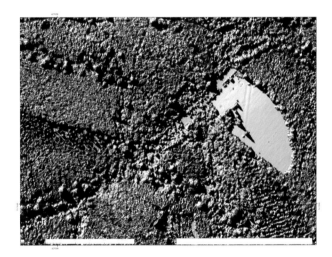

Before and after tree cover stripped away by LiDAR to reveal earthworks

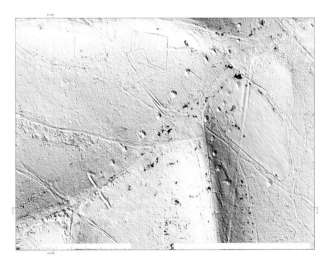

Copyright - Peter Crow, Forest Research. Reproduced by permission

Other evidence

Modern **geophysical survey** equipment can be used to detect changes in moisture levels or magnetic fields, which can indicate hidden signs of past disturbance of the soil such as burning, old ditches or walls. However it can be harder to use in amongst lots of trees with their spreading roots and other vegetation.

Metal detectors may find hidden objects but should only be used with the landowner's consent and away from protected areas. NB - It is an offence to use a metal detector on a Scheduled Monument or on National Trust land.

Portable Finds

Portable Finds or artefacts should be reported to the local museum service or the county archaeologist. They are the property of the landowner except if made of gold or silver, when they are covered by the **1997 Treasure Act** and should be reported to the coroner.

The **Portable Antiquities Scheme** can help identify and record finds, contact your county archaeologist or local museum for more information.

Remember it is the exact location and context of the find that is important historically and this information is essential if the object is to be understood. The value of the object can be greatly reduced without this context.

Documents and maps

Archives such as rentals, surveys and court records can all be important sources of information. Tithe maps of the mid 19th century and some early estate maps are useful in helping to identify some ancient features, including boundary banks, old tracks and change in extent of woodland. Estate documents and records, such as wills and account books, may also provide valuable information.

First edition ordnance survey maps and the surveyors drawings provide a very detailed record from the 19th century. The study of early maps can be particularly important as it may reveal how old woods are. The County Record Office is a good starting point for research. Much information can now also be found on websites.

Old photographs can be studied on websites such as "Sharing Wycombe's Old Photographs" on the Bucks County Council site and Oxfordshire's Heritage Search.

Word of mouth should not be ignored, many locals may know of features within the wood but not necessarily what they are! For example some local residents remember collecting water from the old well in Bottom Wood during the 1920's drought. They also remember collecting blackberries to send to London during the Second World War, which indicates the growth of brambles following felling in 1940. However memories can also become muddled over time, so other evidence may be needed to confirm recollections.

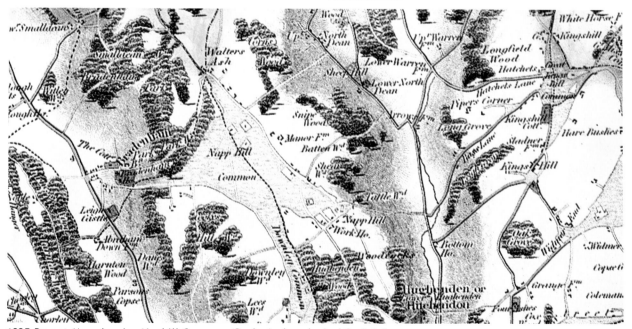

1825 Bryant Map showing Naphill Common (Bucks Archaeological Society)

Historic Features Found in Chiltern Woods

Linear features

Banks & ditches are often important features and may indicate the edge of an estate, a parish or a county. These have legal significance as they were created to show the position of the ownership boundary. This importance can last for hundreds of years, as when a property changes hands the boundary remains unless the land is sold to the neighbour. Marker stones may sometimes be found and should be retained in situ.

Ancient woods often have sinuous or curving boundaries. Straight hedges and fences are more likely to be a feature of planned enclosure after about 1700AD.

Drainage ditches are rarely a feature of woods in the Chilterns due to the woods being on well drained hilltops. Most ditches in Chiltern woods do not have a drainage function, they are there as boundary markers or historically to help keep animals on one side of the bank. Modern run off drains from roads sometimes cut through older banks and ditches. Modern ditches alongside woodland tracks or forest roads may be part of a standard drainage design.

The boundary bank is often a significant feature and frequently had a ditch on the non-woodland side. This was used to keep stock out of the wood. The shape of the boundary is important and gives considerable character to the landscape of the area. In the Chilterns the boundary may have moved over time, with fields being cut out of woods and wood edges spilling back into the fields so that a boundary bank may now be inside the edge of the existing wood. These features may date back hundreds or even thousands of years!

The boundaries of many woods became fixed during the medieval period. Assarting was the small scale clearance of woodland to create fields for agriculture which probably ended during this period.

Bank with ditch inside the wood, Pepperboxes Wood

In some places in the Chilterns the ditch is on the inside of the woodland boundary bank, which has the remnants of a hedge on top. The reason for the ditch being inside the bank is not clear - perhaps to keep animals in the wood? It may just have been for convenience when defining the edge of woods from fields on hillsides.

Former beech hedge on boundary bank, Seer Wood

Banks and ditches

Grim's Ditch, which occurs in many parts of the Chilterns, is a massive early earthwork, although its significance is not fully understood. Stretches have been identified at Pitstone Hill, (Bucks) from Berkhamsted to Wiggington (Herts), from Wendover to Great Missenden, Great Hampden and Bradenham (Bucks) and there are other stretches from Crowmarsh to Nettlebed (Oxon). These are not all the same and probably different stretches date from different periods.

Parish, estate & hundred boundaries can be very significant features, with large banks and deep ditches several metres across. The bounds may have been walked for centuries and ancient trees and other landmarks noted in old documents.

The Black Hedge between Princes and Monks Risborough is a famous local example mentioned in Saxon charters. It can still be traced as a major landscape feature today, part of which runs through more recent woodland.

Buckinghamshire County Council own Pavis, Northhill and Black Woods, a linked group of ancient woodlands on the scarp which cross into three parishes, and have the county boundary with Hertfordshire on one edge. Black wood is in Aston Clinton parish, Northhill Wood is in Buckland parish and Pavis Wood is in Drayton Beauchamp parish. The Hertfordshire County Boundary runs above an ancient hollow way on the eastern edge of the wood. Narrow strip parishes are an ancient feature of the Vale/Chilterns scarp as resources were shared out in medieval (and earlier) times. The parishes of Drayton Beauchamp, Buckland and Aston Clinton are only a few hundred metres wide as they come up from the

Parish boundary, Black and Northhill Woods

Map of Pavis Wood showing parish boundaries

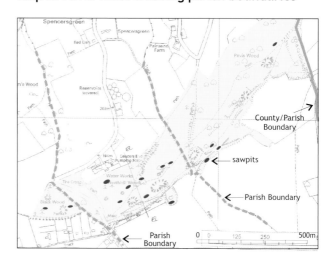

Vale onto the Chilterns plateau. Drayton Beauchamp nearest the Hertfordshire border was in the separate Cotteslow Hundred (a medieval administration unit). I carried out a survey of visible features in these woods and could trace the parish boundaries, identify deep hollow ways, old chalk pits and a line of sawpits as well as woodland boundary banks.

Boundaries of Commonland

These are substantial often sinuous banks, with a ditch on the common side.

Deer park boundaries, also known as the park pale are major banks and ditches which would have had a wood fence or pale on top to keep deer in the park. These were often circular in outline, but this may have expanded or contracted over time. Deer leaps were sometimes created to allow escaped deer to get back into the park. Later landscaped or ornamental parks may not have kept deer so have a less well defined boundary. One example is at Stonor on the Bucks/Oxon border where fallow deer are still kept within a part of the former parkland.

Internal wood banks can also be important but are usually much smaller in size and may divide ownership or indicate compartment units. In the past some blocks would have been leased to a woodsman to use for a limited period. They may also indicate other historic land uses.

Pigotts Wood at North Dean has good examples, indicating changes in ownership and land management over the centuries.

Pigotts Wood Banks

I have been studying Pigotts Wood, North Dean, about four miles north of High Wycombe, Bucks, since 1997.

Dr Tim Southern and Sue Gibson, in April 2008, measured the banks using a laser level with measurements at half metre intervals.

Pigotts Wood – Bank profiles

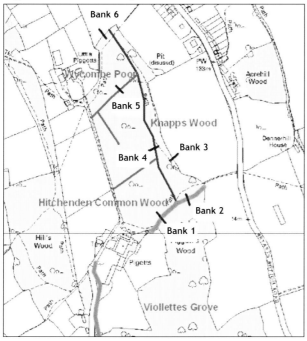

The following profiles show the sizes of banks and ditches, in metres, at the six locations shown on the map of the wood, all drawn to same scale.

Bank 1 top of hill – largest and earliest wood bank - 7.5 metres across and 1 metre high

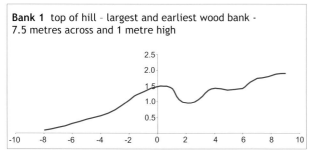

Bank 3 lower edge of wood, ditch inside wood. Similar banks are found on western edge of area on map shown as Viollettes Grove (name of this area in 1646) and likely to be medieval assarted fields. Field is below the bank.

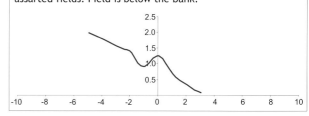

Bank 4 Knapps Wood (internal wood bank and ditch) - runs length of wood to meet the major bank – 6 acres of wood first identified in a sale document of 1559.

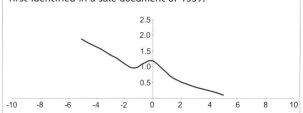

Dr Tim Southern has also investigated boundary banks in South Oxfordshire for the Special Trees and Woods project. In particular he has been following a boundary bank around Wyfold Grange thought to have been created by the Cistercian monks of Thame Abbey in the 13th century.

Old field hedges may also become incorporated within woodland, particularly in more recent plantations on farmland outside the ancient woodland boundary. These hedge banks may be of considerable historical or ecological interest. Seer Wood at North Dean shows periods of woodland expansion into fields.

Ancient coppiced hornbeam in hedge

Former woodland outlines

Some hedges and small woods may be surviving remnants of larger ancient woods that have been partially cleared. These are sometimes shown on old maps. One example are the fields between Bottom Wood and Beacons Bottom near Stokenchurch where a wood, known as Newell's Wood existed in 1842 and is shown on the Tithe Map but was cleared for agriculture during the 19th century. The outline of the wood is now traceable because the boundary hedges and lynchets survive.

Another example a little closer to Stokenchurch is of a small wood now separated from the main body of

East Wood by fields. On the far edge of the wood is a major woodland boundary bank, but there are no banks on the side closest to East Wood. There are however deep quarries and these may have made clearance of this part of the wood difficult, so it survives.

Field systems can sometimes be identified within woods, either small, rectangular fields or old strip lynchets forming terraces on a hillside. A good example is in the Chiltern Society's Bottom Wood, which shows that this area is secondary woodland, although ancient, i.e. over 400 years old, that has grown up on former strip fields.

Evidence of medieval ridge and furrow field management can sometimes be found within woods. Ploughing open fields formed these features over many years.

Flints and stones may be cleared from a field and piled up in a bank or hedge.

Changes in woodland cover over time

Bottom Wood, Radnage

(from Bottom Wood - A Chiltern Woodland)

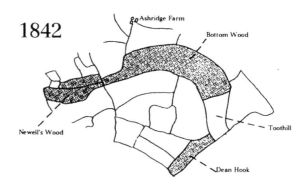

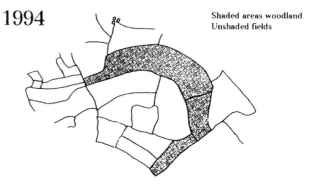

Lynchets

Tracks

Lynchets are steep banks created by ploughing arable hillsides. There are two types:
a) Negative lynchet, where ploughing has cut into the ground, which can over time cause a sizeable drop in level. This may occur on the lower edge of a wood where ploughing cuts close to the hedge.
b) Positive lynchet, where the material loosened by ploughing and erosion piles up, perhaps at a hedge or lower field boundary.

Lynchets vary in size from just a few centimetres to a couple of metres or more. Ploughing may have eroded away old boundary ditches so that the lower edge of the wood is now a steep bank, often with whitebeam, field maple and shrubs that grow on thin chalk soils where there is plenty of light.

Lynchets produced by ploughing on hillside

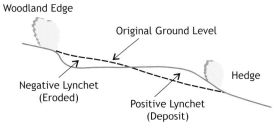

Lynchet

Old trackways may be ancient routes that have been abandoned but many others are still in use as footpaths, bridleways and roads. They are important features of the Chilterns and may indicate many hundreds of years use, bringing stock or wood-fuel up and down hills. They indicate historic links between places.

Many have become adopted as metalled highways but are none the less still important features and require careful management.

Ancient track on the Hardwick Estate

Hill forts

The Ridgeway and the Icknield Way, along the foot of the Chiltern scarp, are thought to be amongst the oldest known routes in England.

At least two major Roman Roads cross the Chilterns, Akeman Street (now A41 in places from Tring to Berkhamsted) and Watling Street (now A5 from St Albans to Dunstable) but these follow valleys and are not found in the woods.

Green Lanes are old unsurfaced routes, which were often used for driving livestock to market. They may have parallel hedges or banks and ditches where they pass through woods.

Old Hollow Ways are sunken eroded routes up hills; many such routes climb up the Chiltern scarp. In places a series of eroded routes has evolved, perhaps to allow traffic to pass in either direction or because one route became impassable. A deep hollow way on the edge of Cut Throat Wood, Holtspur near Beaconsfield, is said to have been a favourite place for attacks by highwaymen. It was replaced by a new turnpike road, which is now the A40.

Pulpit Hill

These Iron Age enclosures are normally circular or oval in shape and often located on top of prominent hills with large banks and ditches. Most of these hillforts are Scheduled Ancient Monuments. Most would originally have been constructed in open grassland, but many are now found within woods. There are about a dozen examples in the Chilterns. Good examples can be visited at Boddington Hill in Wendover Woods, at Cholesbury and at Pulpit Hill near Princes Risborough. West Wycombe Hill has another and others exist above the River Thames, for example at Medmenham.

Sharpenhoe Clappers hillfort

The Cultural Heritage of Woodlands in the Chilterns

Woodland enclosures

Of particular interest in many woods are rectangular enclosures, defined by surviving earthworks, both banks and ditches. Some of these sites have been scheduled as ancient monuments but in some case it is only the largest bank and ditch of the enclosure that has been identified, not the surrounding earthworks and the wider countryside context.

Were these enclosures features of a more open landscape, or do they in fact relate to the woodland more closely than has been realised? Some may be Iron Age, some medieval. Iron working seems to be associated with some of these enclosures, while others may possibly have been constructed to hold livestock.

Old settlements may in some cases be delineated by a bank and ditch. They can indicate settlements of various types such as early farms. Medieval settlements and other enclosures of unknown age are found in several woods. Jenkins Wood is one example near Great Missenden, and there are other enclosures nearby. The drawing is of an enclosure near Marlow investigated by the ROMADAM project.

Old settlements

Warren Wood Earthworks
Hachured Graphic showing inner and outer enclosures
Drawing by John Laker, Archaeology In Marlow, ROMADAM Project

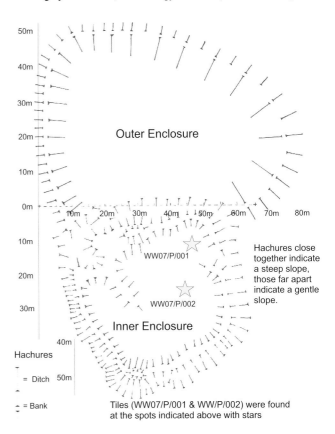

Outer Enclosure

Hachures close together indicate a steep slope, those far apart indicate a gentle slope.

WW07/P/001

WW07/P/002

Inner Enclosure

Hachures

- = Ditch

- = Bank

Tiles (WW07/P/001 & WW/P/002) were found at the spots indicated above with stars

Medieval enclosure bank and ditch near Great Missenden

Mounds

Building platforms are raised level areas that sometimes remain when a building has been abandoned. They may contain the remains of old walls and other materials.

Milestones on old routeways were placed to show distances between towns to help travellers.

Marker stones

These may be placed to help mark out property boundaries, or to show where woodland compartments change. Blocks of puddingstone can be found in a couple of places on the boundary of Pigotts Wood.

Puddingstone in Pigotts Wood

Barrows or burial mounds are surprisingly rare in the Chilterns compared with other chalk areas. Bronze Age barrows can sometimes be found in woodland – this is likely to indicate that the wood has grown up after the barrow was constructed.
A Neolithic barrow has been identified near Beaconsfield. Trees on top of this mound were cleared to protect it from damage.

A Prospect mound is a viewing point to watch hunting, perhaps with a building on top.

Windmills may also have been built on a mound but these are unlikely to be found in ancient woods.

Interpreting the sequence of events

The inter-relationship between old fields, hedges, banks and tracks is very important in identifying the historic sequence of land use. This can be seen for example where a hollow way track cuts through an earlier bank. Another example is where a bank runs up to but does not cross an earlier feature.

Mound in Park Wood, Bradenham

Historic Woodland Management features

Iron Slag and bloomeries

In recent years a number of woods in the Chilterns have been found to contain iron waste from small scale smelting activities. Some of these are thought to date back to the Iron Age and Roman period. The reason they are in woods is that perhaps 60 tonnes of wood was needed to smelt a tonne of iron ore. The wood had to be converted to charcoal first so that it would burn hot enough to produce molten iron in simple clay kilns known as bloomeries.

Iron slag from Pigotts Wood

It was much easier to bring the iron to the wood for it to be worked than to carry bulky and friable charcoal to the iron. It is estimated that roughly 10 tonnes of charcoal are needed to smelt a tonne of iron ore, and about 6 tonnes of wood to make one tonne of charcoal, so a lot of wood is needed for each tonne of ore worked. Clay would also be required to make a bloomery kiln, a simple sort of oven heated with a bellows, and possibly some chalk to mix with the iron ore to help it separate. The iron slag discovered so far seems to date from the Iron Age and Romano-British periods, although it is probable that some is early medieval. Some of the slag found in Pigotts Wood, for example, still has the baked red clay lining from the bloomery attached to it, while other pieces are heavy fragments of the once molten metal.

Recent information from the county archaeologists on the known distribution of Iron Slag sites in the

Iron slag in a woodland enclosure

Chilterns indicates that there are 9 sites in the Bulbourne/Ashridge area of Hertfordshire (of 12 sites known in the county), and 35 sites in Bucks, mainly north and east of High Wycombe. These sites are often in woodlands and some are linked to enclosures in the Wye and Misbourne valleys. A few sites are known in Bedfordshire near Dunstable, but there are no known sites (yet) in the Oxfordshire Chilterns.

Iron slag may indicate former iron smelting sites using locally produced charcoal. A possible source for the iron is the Greensand ridge a few miles north of the Chilterns, with mines known from the Leighton Buzzard (Beds) area, which is accessible to the Bulbourne valley.

Charcoal hearths

Charcoal production was never as important in the Chilterns as some other parts of the country, however there is evidence in some woods of charcoal platforms where burning took place. Most of this use is likely to have been replaced by coal in the early 1800s when canals and later rail could transport coal cheaply around the country.

Black charcoal dust in upturned root plate –
the age of the tree may indicate that charcoal burning took place over 200 years ago.

Charcoal hearths are not the easiest feature to recognise, and are very difficult to photograph! Charcoal used to be burnt in turf covered mounds. The hearths are level circular patches that have often been cut into the hillside to create a flat base, or shallow depression. If it is a charcoal hearth then you are likely to find that the soil is blackened by the remains of charcoal dust which colours your fingers black when rubbed (a different colour to nearby woodland soil). There may be lumps of charcoal remaining – these are most likely to be found on the lower edge of the circle. They are an indication of an important former use of woodland, which was related to other industries such as smelting or gunpowder production. Some local examples are about 5 or 6 metres across, with the levelled area cut into the slope and built up on the lower edge.

Charcoal hearth in Pigotts Wood

Charcoal Burners' huts

Charcoal needed to be tended continuously for a few days when it was being cooked (rather than burnt) to ensure that it did not burn fiercely or go out. Charcoal burners would have had temporary shelters near to the hearths so they could keep an eye on

them. These may well have been small turf covered structures; one possible moss covered ring has been found close to the charcoal hearths in Pigotts Wood.

Bodgers' huts

Bodgers making chair legs in the woods often had their lathes set up in simple wooden shelters, but little visible evidence of this now remains. It may be possible for experts to identify some of these old hut sites from evidence of postholes or enrichment of the soil from all the sawdust and waste shavings piled nearby. Perhaps some of the sheets of corrugated iron sometimes found in woods are the remnants of old huts. Old photographs show these as woodland workshops which were often covered in wood shavings to add a thatch, perhaps to keep the bodgers warm as they worked.

The Chilterns used to be the main centre in England for chair making and other furniture. This was centred in and around High Wycombe. Thousands of people were involved from around 1790 when the existing cottage industry took off, coinciding with the industrial revolution, and numerous small factories and workshops were built to assemble the parts turned in the woods.

Bodgers making chair legs, Great Hampden - photo courtesy Wycombe Museum

Pits and hollows

Be aware of the possibility that vertical shafts for mines or wells may be hidden or partly covered and therefore dangerous! The old well in Bottom Wood is now capped with concrete, but others may not be!

Ancient chalk mine, Boxmoor

Sawpits are a characteristic feature of ancient woods of the Chilterns and indicate a high forest landscape with numerous tall trees to be cut into planks and beams, rather than coppice. These oval pits are normally dug so that they are aligned along the contour, with all the material from the pit piled on the downhill side to make a level platform. A wooden frame would then have been constructed above the pit to hold the log. Most pits are roughly 4 metres or so long by about 2 metres wide. Trees have often grown on the mound or edges of the pit since they were used. The exact use of such every day features was rarely documented.

Sawpit

Sawpits

The following quote is from Pehr Kalm a Finnish visitor to the Chilterns in 1745, translated by Prof Mead: "Sawing sites, where trunks of trees and logs were sawn into boards, are to be found on most English farms. They are made in a very handy way. While in Sweden we have sawyers'

Using a sawpit
Drawing by Joanna Morris

trestles, onto which logs must be lifted with considerable difficulty before they are sawn. Here, it is the practice to dig a saw pit more or less a fathom deep into the ground. The length of the pit is usually 3 or 4 alnar, its breadth 1.5 to 2. (Alnar is a Swedish measure of arm length outstretched to finger tips). On each side, it is lined with boards, so that earth does not fall down into it. The saws that are commonly used here have a broad blade with a handle at either end. One man stands down in the pit and the other above it, each holding his end of the saw. If they wish to saw across them the logs are rolled across the pit, if they wish to saw them into boards, they are placed lengthways along the pit. In this way, the need to hoist the logs onto a sawing bench or higher structure is avoided. When a carpenter or any one else buys a whole beech from the woodland or from one of the fields, he first saws it off close to the ground. When the tree is felled, they do not go to the expense of taking the whole tree away but saw it into pieces where it grew, digging a fathom deep pit of one of the shape that has been described, where the tree can be sawn into boards or whatever is needed."

A sawpit at Frieth in 1900 - photo Wycombe Museum

Numerous sawpits can be found in Chiltern woods such as Bottom Wood and Pigotts Wood, yet are rare elsewhere in England. These oval pits allowed 2 man pit saws to be used to cut timber within the wood, near to where the tree was felled. Some woods have many pits, which show that it was easier to dig new pits than move large trees. Sawpits have been used for hundreds of years until the early years of the twentieth century. Many pits have become filled with soil, leaf litter and other debris. Some were filled in after use. In some cases the pits are shallower and may have only allowed one person standing on the log to cut the timber.

The top dog was the top sawyer who stood above the log and guided the saw along the timber, while the underdog had the dirty job in the pit. The dogs were the metal hooks that held the timbers on to a frame. The long saws had a handle that could be removed to adjust its position. It must have been very hard work,

yet easier to create pits than move the trees far within the wood. Little was wasted, and timber was more valuable than it is today. The nature of Chiltern soils is important, as because of this these pits do not fill with water nor do the sides collapse. It is not clear how frequently these pits were used or reused. Sawpits are relatively rare in many other parts of the country where coppicing was more frequent or where the soil would fill any holes with water!

Lye or Potash Pits were used to burn bracken and branches to produce a fine ash, potash, that could then be used to create a liquid known as lye that was used as a soap. Potash was also important in glass making and as a fertiliser/soil conditioner. One or two possible examples have been seen in the Chilterns – they are almost circular pits, sometimes 'Q' shaped with a stoke hole in one side for stirring the embers to make sure they burn evenly to a fine ash.

Tree throw pits are the result of storm damage uprooting trees. This was a common occurrence across the Chilterns in 1987 and 1990 and many mature beech were blown over. Beech and birch tend to rot away fairly quickly. The result is a D shaped depression with a mound where the tree root plate used to be. In some cases with oak the root plate remains and the soil has been weathered away. The tree throw pit depends on the wind direction (not lined up along the contour like a sawpit). You sometimes find a series of variable sized pits close to each other, from one to four metres across, where trees have fallen "like dominoes".

A possible lye pit at Low Scrubs

Remains of a root plate from storm damage

Quarries

Flint, chalk, sand, gravel and clay pits are found on woods and commons and were an important source of raw materials. Small quarries are frequently found in woods in the Chilterns. Some are very shallow where surface deposits have been removed. Most are steep sided and irregular in shape but frequently have a low entrance point so cart loads of the material could be extracted. Sometimes there are obvious tracks leading from the quarry. The material was for use in local buildings or for road mending.

The quarries reflect the very varied geology of the hills. Denner Hill stone is a surface deposit of very local hard siliceous stone, found north of High Wycombe, which was dug out in some woods and used for building. Other hard forms of chalk known as Totternhoe Stone and Clunch, and also flint were used in local buildings.

Chalk would also have been quarried for liming fields as a soil improver. In the Chilterns this seems to have been spread as chalk rather than cooked in a kiln to make lime.

A woodland quarry

Quarry entrance

Remains of brick kilns at Cadmore End Common

Map showing brickworks on Cadmore End Common 1920s

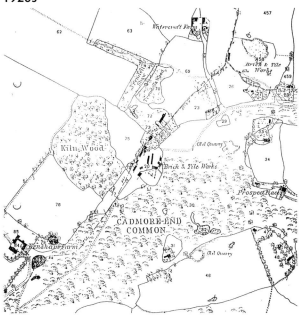

Brick and tile making were medieval industries in the Chilterns using wood for fuel. Local deposits of brick-earth or fire clay, suitable for commercial brickmaking, were found in some woods. For over a hundred years in 13th and 14th Century decorative floor and roofing tiles were made on the edge of commonland at Penn and Tylers Green, supplying orders of over 100,000 tiles for Windsor Castle as just one example. Penn Tiles were made for grand houses and churches around the country. Over 15 kilns have been found so far around Penn. The sites of old kilns should be protected.

Tile making and later brick making were major activities on Nettlebed Common for about 700 years.

In Victorian times there were in the region of a hundred local brickworks using raw materials of brickearth and wood fuel to help build the expanding towns, such as Reading. Clayfield Copse at Caversham shows the results of digging clay for brickmaking, the brickworks was the other side of the road. Chalk was mined beneath this wood to get lime for mortar.

Flooded swallow hole near Lane End

There are still three active brick works surviving today near Chesham.

Swallow holes are caused by natural erosion of the chalk by water; they are often more regular in shape than quarries and lack an extraction point. A particularly fine example near Moorend Common, Lane End, Bucks is fed by a couple of small streams which disappear underground in the swallow hole; this floods in wet weather.

Wells and springs such as the deep well, now capped with concrete, in Bottom Wood owned by the Chiltern Society, are other examples of features that should be identified and retained, but may have safety implications,

A pond in Spring Wood (Oxon) may have been created for ice to form so it could be collected. The remains of an old ice house survives in Walkwood, Beaconsfield.

Brick kiln at Nettlebed

Victorian well building in Spring Wood

Wartime features

Pullingshill Wood First World War Training Trenches
2005 Plan showing Temporary Bench Marks (TBMs)

Drawing by John Laker, Archaeology In Marlow, ROMADAM Project

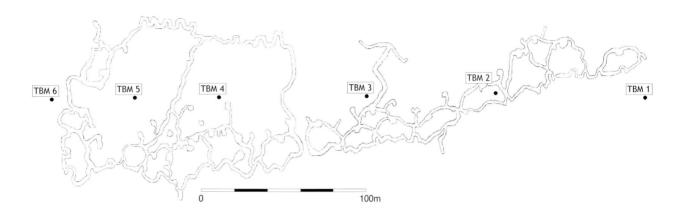

TBM 6   TBM 5   TBM 4   TBM 3   TBM 2   TBM 1

0   100m

A number of woods in the Chilterns were used for a variety of purposes during the two World Wars. The trees were used to hide facilities from aerial reconnaissance and attack. This has left a variety of concrete bases, roads, shelters, pits and trenches, which can be hard to interpret. Careful consideration should be given and advice sought before these features are removed or damaged.

The trenches in Pullingshill Wood, next to Marlow Common, is probably a nationally important archaeological feature and is one of the best preserved practice trench complexes surviving in this country from the First World War.

Volunteers from local group "Archaeology in Marlow" have mapped some 1400 metres of trenches, which they believe were originally about 2 metres deep and 2 metres wide, and associated features. The trenches were dug in 1915 by the Grenadier Guards and local people for military training based at Bovingdon Green Camp in 1915 and 1916.

Another fine example of trenches can be found on Berkhamsted Common, part of the Ashridge Estate. A smaller scale feature can be found in the woods at Whiteleaf Hill, Bucks.

Bomb craters can sometimes be found, e.g. in the wood next to Denham airfield, as can craters from wartime plane crashes, including one at Brush Hill above Princes Risborough.

First World War trenches in Pullingshill Wood

Other features found in woods will in time develop greater historical or cultural significance and should not necessarily be cleared away.

Second World War storage near Checkendon

Many archaeological sites are no longer visible, as the evidence of past activity may be buried in the soil. Many features have yet to be discovered! Much evidence of archaeological interest is to be found very close to the surface and so is very vulnerable to disturbance. Wet areas can be useful because they may hold dateable layers of deposits with ancient pollen grains, which can be used to interpret the vegetation and environment of earlier centuries.

The exact location and position of any artefacts, such as pottery, is critical to understanding the items' significance, so these should be left undisturbed in situ, and reported to the county archaeologists.

White helleborine

Vegetation can be an important clue to the historic use of an area. Changes in vegetation can pick out a variety of features such as old banks and ditches, where different soil and moisture characteristics allow different plants to grow. Mosses for example are often found on old boundary banks, as the soil conditions here are different to the surrounding woodland. Sometimes plants such as bluebells fail to spread even quite modest distances if a bank makes it difficult for the seeds to cross. This can be a clue to the age of the woodland. A number of species have been identified by English Nature as indicators of ancient woods in the Chilterns (see list in Appendix). The greater the number of these species that occur on a site, the more likely it is to be ancient (but other factors such as soil type are also important).

Old fire sites change the soil and are colonised by different mosses and plants such as willowherb. Stinging nettles and elm often indicate enriched or disturbed ground around habitation and may remain dominant as evidence of former activities for perhaps hundreds of years. Some rare plants can be associated with archaeological features, birdsnest orchid and violet helleborine are a couple of rare woodland species sometimes found on these features.

The **Historical Ecology** of woodlands is a fascinating subject and is worth further study in the Chilterns. Living features should not be ignored when considering the history of a wood. Trees are particularly long-lived plants and can tell us much about the recent past and may be indicators of earlier land uses. Even if individual plants themselves do not live long, the fact that their offspring have survived may indicate a long continuity of stable habitat conditions.

Old hedges often contain a wide range of trees and shrubs and acquire more species with age, but this depends on the soil type and degree of shade. These hedges should be retained but are likely to require management such as coppicing or laying. Careful consideration should be given to the position of any fencing. Do not cut corners, the irregular shapes of ancient boundaries are important in giving these ancient Chiltern woods their character, and are historically significant in their own right. Many simple straight thorn hedges were planted in recent centuries as a result of Enclosure Acts.

Ancient trees

Hornbeam stub hedges are a special feature of many woodland edges in the Buckinghamshire and Hertfordshire Chilterns and are rare elsewhere. Some are very old. They require careful management to conserve them. This might include careful high coppicing of the stub to prevent its collapse and removal of surrounding trees to give it the light it needs. Shade and animal damage are threats to the survival of these old woodland boundary hedges.

Pollards result from an ancient form of woodland management in which branches were cut to provide fodder and firewood, allowing new shoots to grow out of reach of browsing animals. Some of the oldest trees, known as veterans, have considerable cultural and ecological importance. They are found either as boundary trees or on old wooded commons, where they were on grazing land, i.e. former "wood pasture". In some cases these trees have survived for several hundred years to become historic features in their own right. Burnham Beeches and Frithsden Beeches are classic examples of pollarded woodland.

Pollarded beech, Naphill Common

Other Notable Trees either individuals or groups, which are traditional landmarks or are of historical interest should be retained in their setting. Some trees are named features, such as the King Oak at Latimer, a magnificent old tree that was recently saved from felling. However the Queen Beech in the same wood blew over in a storm a few years ago. The Project discovered the largest rowan in the country in a beech wood near Chesham in 1995 when it was 28 metres tall and had a diameter of 56cm measured 1.3m above the ground.

Hornbeam boundary hedge near Chorleywood

Veteran Trees

Veteran trees with their holes and hollows resulting from decay and lost branches are of particular value for rare wildlife, including bats, beetles and fungi. They are also of considerable historical interest and as landmarks. The girth of old trees is normally measured at 1.5 metres from the ground. Many examples of interesting trees are recorded as part of our Special Trees and Woods project and found on the Chilterns AONB website.

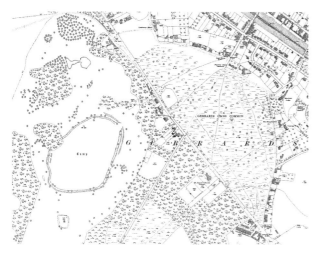

1925 Ordnance Survey Map of Bulstrode Camp

Bulstrode Camp

Examples of Special Trees can be seen at Bulstrode Camp, an Iron Age hillfort in Gerrards Cross, Bucks. The Gerrards Cross parish council website says "On a hill south-east of the House, there is a very large circular entrenchment ... with some large old oaks growing on its banks" quoting George Lipscomb from The History and Antiquities of the County

Bricked up oak

of Buckingham Vol. VIII (1847). One hundred and sixty years later these old oak trees, several measuring over 5 metres in circumference, have an archaeological interest as an example of early tree conservation. The hollow trunks were bricked up in 1900 to try to protect them (not now considered a good practice) but the trees are still there.

Veteran oak at Bulstrode Camp, Gerrards Cross

Pigotts Wood

Pigotts Wood, North Dean near High Wycombe, Bucks

This is a particularly well documented woodland. Documentary evidence for parts of this wood go back to 1559 in papers held at the Bucks Record Office in Aylesbury. It has been used by the Chiltern Woodlands Project for over ten years for woodland archaeology training events, so is now well known.

Pigotts Wood, North Dean, Bucks

Based on 1874 map and showing some of the tracks through the wood. With thanks to Nicola Bannister

⊤⊤⊤	Major bank and ditch
⊤⊤⊤	Smaller bank and ditch
▼▼▼	Lynchet
▲▼▲	Quarry
⌣	Sawpit
C	Charcoal hearth
⋅⋅⋅⋅	Tracks

The earliest reference is for the sale of a six acre parcel of land within Huchynden Common Wood next to a five acre piece of the wood owned by the Dean and Chapter of Chichester. This land was later left in a will by a local wheelwright to his sister in 1703. Later a turner in Great Hampden transferred the land by deed poll to his younger son.

In 1592 part of the southern end of the wood known as Vyollettes Grove was left in a will to a cousin.

In 1654 three and a half acres of common waste in Hughenden Common Wood were marked and bounded by great stones and sold.

This is interesting because the names of the wood have changed over time and it is subdivided into smaller ownerships bounded by banks, which can be traced today *(see maps)*.

Pigotts Wood contains a range of features of interest. Some of the bank profiles have been measured by Tim Southern and Sue Gibson *(see photos and graphs on page 27)*. The banks are of varying sizes, some with the ditch on the inside of the woodland.

The sawpits have also been plotted both as a sketch map and using GPS.

Pigotts Wood - GPS plots

Red dots sawpits, black dots charcoal, green dots quarries

Survey Feb 2007

Charcoal hearths have been identified, including the possible site of a charcoal burners hut.

The wood has a number of small quarries and the 1851 census showns one of the residents of Pigotts Common listed as a sandstone cutter. There are documents giving the rights to cut the local hard Denner Hill stone within the wood. Pigotts Common was a late enclosure in 1857.

Iron slag has been found in two areas of the wood, one area at least has evidence for being the site of a bloomery to smelt iron, as the slag has clay lining attached to it from the bloomery kiln.

Sawpit

Bottom Wood

Bottom Wood, Radnage, Bucks is owned by the Chiltern Society.

I have organised management of this ancient wood since 1983. It lies near the now enclosed Radnage Common and its lower edge is the parish boundary between Stokenchurch and Radnage parishes. This boundary is a double bank in places. The wood was partially felled in 1940 and has since regenerated.

Interesting features in this wood include a well now capped in concrete, which was used by local villagers in the 1920's drought. A hollow way leads down the edge of the wood to this well.

Wooded hillside

A feature in the wood that is rare in the Chilterns is that the hillside is terraced with four narrow strips of former fields separated by steep lynchets. These strips may possibly have been abandoned after the Black Death in the fourteenth century? It was documented as woodland by the seventeenth century, and has numerous sawpits, mostly in the valley bottom.

Bottom Wood, Radnage
Sketch map of archaeological features drawn by John Morris. December 1998

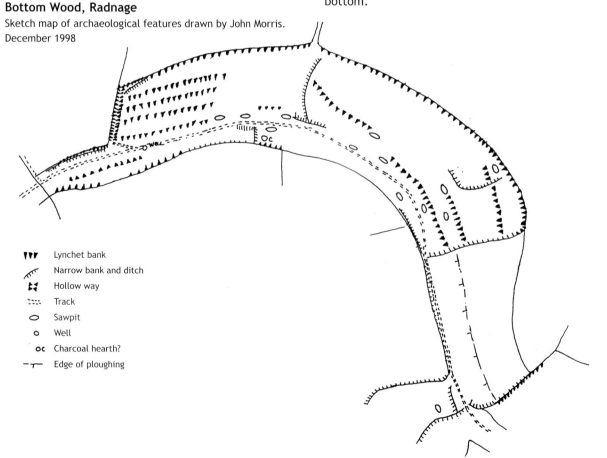

ᵛᵛᵛ	Lynchet bank
	Narrow bank and ditch
	Hollow way
	Track
⬭	Sawpit
○	Well
oc	Charcoal hearth?
	Edge of ploughing

Spring Wood

Spring Wood near Sonning Common, Oxon

This small privately owned wood is full of interesting features. Of particular interest is an old spring which was the water supply for the village and was covered in Victorian times with a brick built structure to protect the well. The spring linked by a channel to a deep 80 metre long trench of unknown purpose. It also links to a shallow pond, banked in to make a square, was this perhaps for collecting ice for an ice house? Or perhaps for washing?

The trench

Ordnance Survey first series 1878

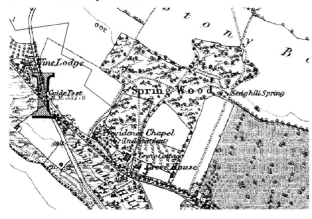

The spring is shown as Sedghill Spring on the first ordnance survey map and the wood had been renamed Spring Wood. The wood was not shown at all on the Jeffreys 1767 map, but this is probably only because they needed to show a sponsors name here! Spring Wood is shown as Legget Copse on the Bryant map of 1823. The wood has remained the same shape since the nineteenth century, as shown on the maps.

Apart from the spring and associated features this wood is also notable for the large number of sawpits, nine found in a 6ha wood, and the fact that its boundaries have changed over time.

Spring Wood
Sketch map of archaeological features drawn by John Morris.

TTTT	Wood bank and ditch
،'/،	Quarry
- - -	Path
vvw	Lynchet
◯	Sawpit
Sp	Spring

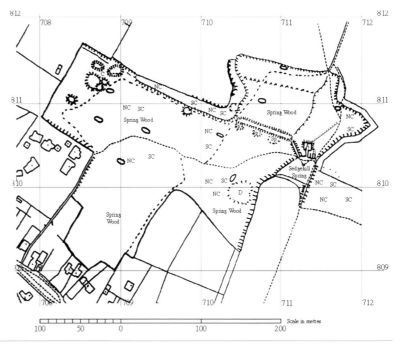

Bradenham Woods

Bradenham Woods Archaeological Survey

With the support of partnership funding from the Sustainable Development Fund the National Trust has been undertaking an intensive survey of archaeological features in woodland in the parish of Bradenham, Bucks.

The project – known as the Bradenham Woods Historic Landscape Survey, involved volunteers working under the direction of the Trust's Regional Archaeologist Gary Marshall. The aim of the project is to map, record and interpret all earthwork features so that an understanding can be developed of features both typical and atypical of Chiltern woodland.

To date, more than 50 sawpits have been mapped in an area covering little more than half a square kilometre. Other typical features include boundary banks and ditches, tracks, and charcoal burning

platforms, whilst slightly unusual features include an enigmatic mound with encircling ditch (possibly a prospect mound associated with the Tudor deer park), and a house platform known as 'the homestead' which on the basis of pottery in the vicinity seems to have a 13th or 14th century origin.

Volunteers surveying the Homestead

The Homestead, Park Wood

Map of the Bradenham Woods Historic Landscape Survey - thanks to Gary Marshall, National Trust

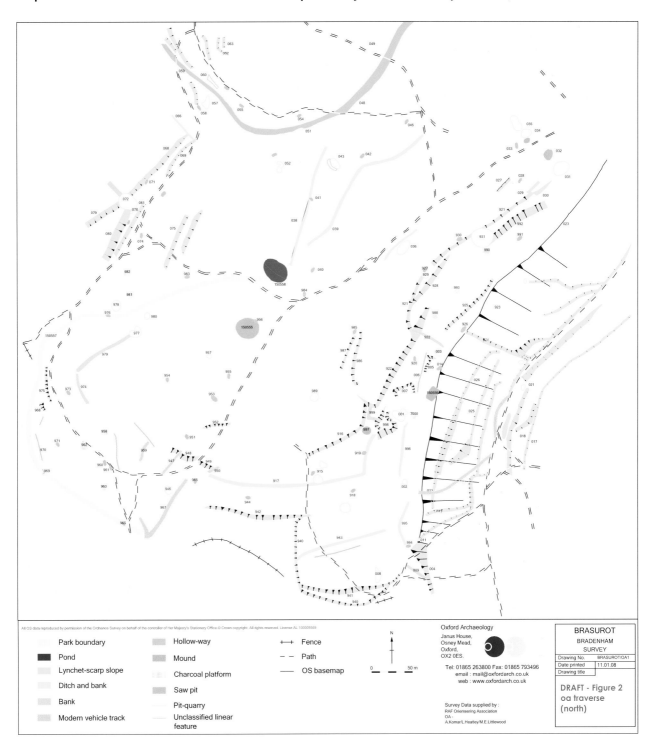

Low Scrubs

Low Scrubs, Ellesborough, Bucks now owned by the National Trust

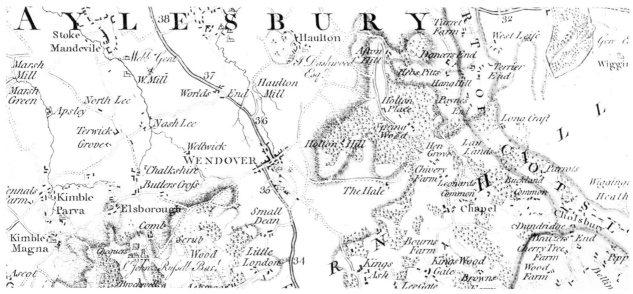

Jeffrey's Map of Bucks 1770. *Low Scrubs is shown as Scrub Wood (Commonland) courtesy Bucks Archaeological Society*

Once part of a large area of common that was enclosed in May 1805, this area was returned to the poor of the parish as a fuel allotment. Two charities were set up to allow the 'poor inhabitants of Ellesborough' to cut wood, furze, fern and other fuels from this area. One feature of interest is a 'Q' shaped pit which may have been used to burn gorse and bracken to create potash.

Villagers lopped branches from scrubby beech using hooks and axes and these may be some of the oldest surviving beech in the Chilterns. This process continued into living memory and our Special Trees and Woods project recorded an oral history with an elderly resident, who remembers how the villagers went about it. He says that families had their own

Special Trees and Woods Project visit to discuss management

Ancient beech coppice

Estate boundary fence embedded in old beech hedge

particular groups of beech that they cut for fuel. It is known that cutting continued to the 1940s.

One sinuous edge of the common is a former hundred boundary. It is still the estate, parish and district boundary. It has remains of the iron railing fence surviving in places where the beech hedge has grown into them so they could not be removed for the war effort.

A laid hornbeam hedge on a bank forms another boundary on two sides of this site; it may date back to the 1805 enclosure.

This site also contains a curious rectangular enclosure with wide bank and ditch but no obvious entrance point, its age and purpose are unknown.

Ancient trackway

How To Care For Historical Features:

Modern forestry equipment

Harvester thinning larch

Until the last century woodland work was labour intensive and removal of cut material was difficult, so timber was often converted in the woods. Modern saws and machinery can now clear woodlands easily, removing vegetation and levelling the many bumps and hollows that give the land its form and character. Compaction by heavy machinery can be a serious problem affecting the soil, drainage, the growth of new trees, vegetation and historical features. Heavy

tractors and trailers may cause ruts, and those with caterpillar tracks dragging felled timber may leave the wood looking as if tanks have driven over it. The choice of equipment on sensitive sites is very important. Wide low-pressure tyres can help spread weight over a wider area reducing the risk of ruts developing.

Identify features and record information
As far as is possible identify sensitive features on a sketch map before any work takes place. A compass can be useful to plot directions. Walking the wood in winter can be a good time to pick out many features when the undergrowth has died down and otherwise hidden features are more visible. Frost, snow and spring vegetation may all pick out subtle variations in soil topography, which could indicate a hidden feature.

Inform contractors and identify locations
Draw up detailed contracts to avoid accidental damage. It is essential to inform the timber buyers and their contractors in a written agreement with a map, and again on site, about features of interest and areas to avoid. Mark off sensitive areas using

Stacking felled conifers for collection by articulated lorry

coloured tape (or similar easily visible markers) so contractors can identify at a glance where they should not go. Do not assume contractors will recognise features if they have not been pointed out to them. It is not always easy to remember these details when driving a machine in the woods!

Marking internal bank with hazard tape

Agree and mark extraction routes

Extraction routes and stacking and loading areas must be carefully planned and machinery restricted to designated routes in work agreements.

Agree and mark extraction routes clearly, especially if they have to cross sensitive areas such as banks. Mats of brash or lop and top can be used to protect features from damage such as rutting. Use existing tracks for extraction where this is appropriate. Keep ground disturbance to a minimum.

Keep stacking and loading areas well away from sensitive locations as these areas are subject to heavy use and compaction.

The creation of new woodland roads and hard standings for timber stacking needs to be very carefully planned to avoid causing damage to both the ecology and archaeology of the woodland.

Use of extraction equipment

Consider using lighter forestry equipment, low ground pressure tyres, or even horse extraction on vulnerable sites, or in part of the wood. Mobile sawmills may also help by converting timber on site.

Timing of work

Aim to carry out work in late summer or autumn, when ground conditions are normally at their driest.

Horse extraction in Angling Spring Wood, Great Missenden

The Cultural Heritage of Woodlands in the Chilterns

If the wood is likely to be harmed in wet weather be prepared to stop work if necessary. Inform any timber buyer or contractor of this possibility when work is agreed! It is difficult to predict or guarantee hard frost in winter so that work can take place.

Position of fences

Take care where fences and gates are placed to ensure that irregular boundaries maintain their character. Fences should not cross archaeological features, such as banks, as this is likely to focus erosion by people or stock close to the fence. Fence posts can also damage stratified deposits.

One of the greatest threats to the appearance of woods in the landscape is through straightening the boundary for the convenience of modern fencing. Fences require straight runs with few strainer posts to keep costs down but if these fences are not carefully planned the ancient boundary can be altered. The result in the landscape is less pleasing on the eye and less valuable historically!

Try to keep fences away from archaeological sites wherever possible.

Old ditches and banks

Sometimes boundary ditches will need to be cleared of infill if the sides have collapsed or matter has accumulated. These ditches should only be cleared if absolutely necessary and work should be carried out sensitively, ideally using hand tools. Remember that

doing nothing is likely to be better for archaeological remains than insensitive work. If mechanical diggers are used it is important to follow the line of the old ditch and not enlarge the ditch by using too big a bucket. Disposing of the spoil on the old bank must also be carried out carefully if the historic feature is to retain its traditional shape and scale. In some cases rare vegetation may be associated with the bank or the ditch; scraping the ditch clean and burying existing vegetation could harm these plants or lead to their loss. Machinery should operate from the field side of the ditch, if the bank is on the inside nearest the wood.

Tree Stumps

Do not level the site or grub out stumps if this is not absolutely necessary. It is far better (and cheaper) to leave tree stumps to rot in situ. In some cases regrowth may not be desirable and treatment with herbicide may be necessary.

Thinning and felling

Any gaps in the canopy will increase light levels to the ground so that natural regeneration of trees and undergrowth is more likely to occur. This young growth may hide any features and create management issues for the future.

Tree planting or restocking

In general terms it is best to avoid planting on archaeological sites as tree roots can cause damage. The most likely exception could be replanting a hedge on top of a boundary bank. However coppicing or laying existing remnants of the old hedge may be more desirable. Do not plant in the ditch or in pits. It is best to keep these areas free from tree and shrub growth and retain them as open features.

Retain existing open spaces and clearings where these have a long history.
On some sites regular cutting, mowing or stock grazing may help keep archaeological monuments open so they can be seen. Clearance of scrub or

Shire Lane holloway, Pavis Wood

developing trees and control of bracken and bramble by cutting or use of selective herbicides may be appropriate in some cases.

Management of old trees

Retain old pollards and veteran trees because of their historical, cultural and nature conservation importance. In some cases some form of tree surgery may be necessary for safety reasons and could help prolong the life of the tree if it is carried out carefully. Often these trees require more light as they can be crowded out and shaded by young vigorous trees. However this sort of work needs to be carried out with great care as rapid changes in the micro climate can result in the death of the tree from stress related to exposure to wind and heat. If veteran trees are to be repollarded then at least some of the living branches should be retained with leaves and buds; they should not be cut hard back to a stump and be expected to survive.

Care of old hedges

Hedges are likely to need management to survive and will need particular care and attention. One of the greatest threats to a hedge is from shading by the overhanging tree canopy, which kills hedge plants and leads to gaps. Secondly, if the hedge gets too tall it may become unstable and fall over. If this happens the trees should be cut off and the stump replaced in its hole to retain the profile of the bank. The height and frequency of cut will depend on the type of hedge and its condition. Ideally mixed hedges should be allowed to grow for a few years between cuts.

Management of old hornbeam stubs

These old stubs are a feature of some Chiltern woodland boundaries (mainly in Buckinghamshire and Hertfordshire) and they may require high coppicing to rejuvenate them and stop them collapsing. They should be cut several centimetres above the height of the last cut. The cut should be made to slope away from the stub. Where possible some live shoots should be retained to stimulate new growth. The best time of year for this work is likely to be from December through to March. The new hedge re-growth may need protection from stock in the field, particularly from horses! Grey squirrels also cause damage. Some stems can be laid over along the bank; these are known as

Natural regeneration on Boddington hillfort, Wendover

pleachers. Shading trees may need to be cleared back to give open canopy of at least 7 metres width along the length of the woodbank.

Animal problems

Animals, particularly rabbits, can undermine historic features with their burrows so that the earthwork collapses. Rabbit numbers may need to be controlled to protect this interest.

Badgers setts could also cause problems in undermining earthworks, but badgers and their setts are protected by law under the 1991 Badgers Act. Consult Natural England for advice.

Human use

Erosion by horse riding, mountain or scramble bikes and other off-road vehicles can cause localised problems and should not be allowed on sensitive archaeological features. This may require careful use of signs or barriers to prevent unwanted disturbance. Erosion can also be caused by livestock gathering under trees for shelter, and by human activity. Feet will often cause more damage on top of banks than in the ditches.

Avoid the temptation to fill hollows and pits with rubbish or stumps and branchwood. Carefully clear away recently dumped material without digging into the original ground level.

Problems of Weather

Trees uprooted by windblow in storms may threaten archaeological evidence, as the root ball can rip up a substantial amount of material. In some circumstances it may be desirable to fell trees to avoid damage to banks. Where root plates have ripped up a bank carefully cut the trunk and tip the root plate back to its original position, where it can decay in situ and retain the bank profile.

Erosion by runoff following heavy rain can be a problem on steep hillsides, particularly if felling leaves bare ground or exposes old sunken hollow ways. However these hollow ways have developed by years of erosion! Existing scars can be enlarged by heavy rain.

Flooding resulting in burial in sediment is one way that remains are preserved under the ground to perhaps be rediscovered by future archaeologists!

Uprooted beech on medieval enclosure bank

Conclusion

It is important that woods are managed sensitively and sustainably. This will help maintain the character of these fascinating woods so that they can be enjoyed by future generations. There is much yet to be discovered in woods across the Chilterns and I hope this book encourages you to look more closely at the various humps and hollows and to speculate about their origin.

But remember, if in doubt about how to manage a wood without causing damage to the archaeological and cultural heritage, get expert advice.

Measuring earthwork near Sarratt

PROTECTING WOODLAND ARCHAEOLOGICAL FEATURES

To help protect and conserve these features:-

- Identify features on the ground before you start felling.

- Remember - avoid damage to any features that have been pointed out to you, especially scheduled monuments!

- It is an offence to damage scheduled monuments! Consult English Heritage.

- Mark off sensitive areas with hazard tape or temporary Heras fencing.

- Always keep to agreed extraction routes and stacking areas.

- Use only the equipment and machinery agreed in any contract with the owners.

- Avoid crossing BANKS AND DITCHES with heavy machinery except at agreed points.

- Protect sensitive features, such as old tracks and ditches, with brash mats etc where they have to be crossed.

- Stop work if weather conditions deteriorate, ie if it gets too wet.

- Avoid damage by machinery to any PITS (large or small).

- Do not fill or excavate any PITS (large or small) with material, unless work is agreed.

- Avoiding planting into archaeological remains such as banks.

- If you discover features or artefacts get advice / consult county archaeologist!

- Keep fencing design to the landform ie fence outside boundary banks and ditch lines - do not straighten out by crossing features.

- Treasure Act (1996) requires certain finds to be reported and the Portable Antiquities Scheme helps identify and record objects - contact the County Museum for more information. (See www.finds.org.uk)

- Record exactly where you find any objects in case further investigation is needed.

Some features are related to woodland management such as boundary banks, sawpits and charcoal hearths.

Other features happen to be in woods and relate to earlier or other activities eg Iron Age Hillforts, quarries, field systems, war time activities.

VETERAN TREES, ANCIENT COPPICE AND OLD HEDGES are all important features of the historic landscape and should be retained where possible. They should be managed sensitively - get expert advice.

Remember the new England Woodland Grant Scheme can pay a grant for assessment of cultural heritage if they consider it necessary. Contact the Forestry Commission for more information see www.forestry.gov.uk Look at the FC Land Information Search section for designated sites or www.magic.gov.uk

John Morris, Chiltern Woodlands Project
The Lodge, 90 Station Road, Chinnor, Oxon OX39 4HA
Tel 01844 355503 email woodlands@chilternsaonb.org

'Make sure you don't destroy hundreds of years of history'

Contacts and websites:

Chilterns Conservation Board www.chilternsaonb.org
The Lodge 90 Station Road, Chinnor, Oxon OX39 4HA
Tel 01844 355500

See www.chilternsaonb.org/woodlandweb
a new interactive website explains more about
woodland history with illustrations by Richard Allen.

Also see www.chilternsaonb.org/special for examples
of trees and woods recorded by the Heritage Lottery
funded Special Trees and Woods Project

Chiltern Open Air Museum, Newlands Park, Chalfont St
Giles, Bucks HP8 4AD 01494 871117 www.coam.org.uk

English Heritage 23 Saville Row, London W1X 1AB 0171
973 3000 www.english-heritage.org.uk

Forestry Commission Upper Icknield Way, Aston Clinton
Aylesbury, Bucks HP22 4RF (South East region – Chilterns
office)

Forestry Commission East England Region Stanton
Downham, Brandon, Suffolk IP27 0TJ   01842 815544

Forestry Commission website has a map based land
information search to check for landuse designations see
www.forestry.gov.uk

For landuse designations, including ancient monuments
see www.magic.gov.uk

Museum of English Rural Life, University of Reading,
Whiteknights, PO Box 229, Reading RG6 6AG 0118 931
8660 http://www.reading.ac.uk/merl/

National Trust Regional Office, Hughenden Manor, High
Wycombe, Bucks HP14 4LA

Natural England Chilterns, North Wessex Downs and
Berkshire Team, 11 Fenlock Court, Blenheim Office Park,
Long Hanborough, Oxford OX29 8LN Tel: 0300 060 1916
www.naturalengland.org.uk

Wycombe Museum, Priory Avenue, High Wycombe, Bucks
HP13 6PX   01494 421895 www.wycombe.gov.uk

Bucks County Archaeologist, Environmental Services,
County Hall, Aylesbury, Bucks HP22 5PJ 01296 395000
www.buckscc.gov.uk

Centre for Buckinghamshire Studies, County Hall, Walton
Street, Aylesbury, Bucks. HP20 1UU Archives: 01296
382587 www.buckscc.gov.uk website includes Sharing
Wycombe's Old Photographs (SWOP)

Hertfordshire County Council Archaeological Service,
Environment Department, County Hall, Hertford SG13
8DN 01992 555244
www.hertsdirect.org/libsleisure/heritage1/archaeology/

Hertfordshire Archives and Local Studies, Register Office
Block, County Hall, Pegs Lane, Hertford SG13 8DQ 01438
737333
www.hertsdirect.org/libsleisure/heritage1/HALS/

Oxford Archaeological Unit, Department of Leisure & Arts,
Central Library, Westgate, Oxford OX1 1DY 01865 810825
www.oxfordshire.gov.uk

Oxfordshire Studies, Central Library, Westgate, Oxford
OX1 1DY 01865 815749 www.oxfordshire.gov.uk
The excellent Heritage Search section has Oxfordshire
County Council's heritage resources for documents,
objects, photographs and publications

Oxfordshire Record Office, St Luke's Church, Temple
Road, Cowley, Oxford OX4 2HT 01865 398200
www.oxfordshire.gov.uk

The counties operate the Portable Antiquities Scheme to
record archaeological objects found by the public and to
broaden awareness and understanding of the past
see www.finds.org.uk

Woodland Trust www.woodland-trust.org.uk includes
management plans for their woods.

Small Woods Association www.smallwoods.org.uk

www.old-maps.co.uk has first edition ordnance survey
maps on line from 1880's and modern aerial photos.

www.visionofbritain.org.uk/travellers/index.jsp gives
details of historic travel writings.

Bibliography and References

Dr Nicola Bannister edited by Patrick McKernan (2007) *The cultural heritage of woodlands in the South East*

Bannister, Nicola R. Surrey County Council (1996) *Woodland Archaeology in Surrey*

Buckinghamshire Archaeological Society (2000) *Buckinghamshire 1760's and 1820's in the county maps of Jeffreys and Bryant*

Buckinghamshire County Council (1992) *A Plan for the Chilterns - Woodland Policy*

Chilterns Conference (1994 & 2005) *Management Plan for the Chilterns AONB - The Framework for Action*

Chilterns Conservation Board (2008) *Management Plan for the Chilterns AONB - The Framework for Action 2008 -13*

Chilterns Conservation Board edited by Melanie Solik (2003 conference) *New Perspectives on Chiltern Landscapes*

Crow, Peter, et al. (2007). *Woodland vegetation and its implications for archaeological survey using LiDAR. Forestry. 80 (3) pp 241-252*

Defra and FC (2005) *Keepers of Time – A statement of policy for England's Ancient and Native Woods*

Defra (2007) *A Strategy for England's Trees, Woods and Forests*

Forestry Commission *Ancient Woodland Inventory* Figures on ancient woodland cover in the Chilterns from Patrick McKernan FC (personal communication)

Forestry Commission Practice Guide (2003) *Restoration of Native Woodland on Ancient Woodland Sites*

Hepple, Leslie & Doggett, Alison (1992) *The Chilterns*

Hornby R.J. & Welsh, J. NCC report (1990) *An Evaluation of the Wildlife Interest of Chiltern Woodlands*

Mabey, Richard (2007) *Beech Combings*

Mead W.R. (2003)   ISBN 1-85065-729-7 *Pehr Kalm - A Finnish Visitor to the Chilterns in 1748*

Morris, John (1999) *History in Chiltern Woods - A guide to the Identification and Management of Woodland Archaeological Features*

Rackham, Oliver (1976) *Trees & woods in the British Landscape*

Rackham, Oliver (1986) *The History of the Countryside*

John Laker editor (2008) *Archaeology in Marlow's ROMADAM Project*

Edited by Ian Rotherham et al. Sheffield Hallam University (2008) *The Woodland Heritage Manual - A guide to investigating wooded landscapes*

Stidworthy John (1994) *Bottom Wood – A Chiltern Woodland*

West Wycombe hillfort, church and mausoleum

Ancient Woodland Plants in the Chilterns

(From An Evaluation of Wildlife Interest of Chiltern woods - NCC 1990)

The following are considered to be strongly associated with ancient woods

Wood: _____ **Grid Ref:** _____ **Date of Survey:** _____

Woody plants

Field maple - Acer campestre
Hornbeam - Carpinus betulus
Midland Hawthorn - Crataegus laevigata
Spurge laurel - Daphne laureola
Mezereon - Daphne mezereon
Holly - Ilex aquifolium
Crab apple - malus sylvestris
Aspen - Populus tremula
Wild cherry - Prunus avium
Sessile Oak - Quercus patrea
Butchers broom - Ruscus aculeatus
Wild Service tree - Sorbus torminalis
Wych Elm - Ulmus glabra
Guelder Rose - Viburnum opulus

Flowering plants

Moschatel - Adoxa moschatellina
Ramsons - Allium ursinum
Columbine - Aqueliga vulgaris
Nettle leaved bellflower - Campanula trachelium
Coralroot - Cardamine bulbifera
Opposite leaved golden saxifrage - Chrysosplenium oppositifolium
Pignut - Conopodium majus
Lily of the Valley - Convallaria majalis
Wood spurge - Euphorbia amygdaloides
Woodruff - Galium odoratum
Green hellebore - Helleborus viridis
Bluebell - Hyacinthoides non-scripta
Tutsan - Hypericum androsaemum
Slender St Johns-wort - Hypericum pulchrum
Stinking Iris - Iris foetidissima
Yellow archaeangel - Lamiastrum galeobdolon
Toothwort - Lathraea squamaria
Bitter-vetch - Lathyrus montanus
Yellow pimpernel - Lysimachia nemorum
Common Cow wheat - Melampyrum pratense
Yellow birdsnest - Monotropa
Wood Sorrel - Oxalis acetosella
Herb Paris - Paris quadrifolia
Barren Strawberry - Potentilla sterilis
Primrose - Primula vulgaris
Goldilocks Buttercup - Ranunculus auricomus
Sanicle - Sanicula europea
Black bryony - Tamus communis
Early Dog violet - Viola reichenbachiana

Ancient Woodland Plants in the Chilterns

(From An Evaluation of Wildlife Interest of Chiltern woods - NCC 1990)

The following are considered to be strongly associated with ancient woods

Wood: _____ Grid Ref: _____ Date of Survey: _____

Orchids

Ghost orchid - Epipogium aphyllum

Broad leaved helleborine - E.helleborine

Narrow lipped helleborine - E.leptochila

Green flowered helleborine - E.phyllanthes

Violet Helleborine - E. pupurata

Birdsnest Orchid - Neottia nidus-avis

Early purple orchid - Orchis mascula

Greater butterfly orchid - Platanthera chlorantha

Grasses etc

Bearded Couch - Agropyron caninum

Hairy brome - Bromus ramosus

Wood small reed - Calamagrostis epigejos

Pale Sedge - Carex pallescens

Pendulous Sedge - Carex pendula

Remote Sedge - Carex remota

Thin Spiked wood sedge - Carex strigosa

Wood sedge - Carex sylvatica

Giant fescue - Festuca gigantea

Creeping Soft grass - Holcus mollis

Wood barley - Hordelymus europeus

Southern Wood rush - Luzula forsteri

Hairy wood rush - Luzula pilosa

Great wood rush - Luzula sylvatica

Wood melick - Melica uniflora

Wood millet - Milum effusum

Wood meadow grass - Poa nemoralis

Ferns

Hard fern - Blechium spicant

Narrow Buckler fern - Dryopteris carthusiana

Scaly male fern   - Dryopteris pseudomas

Harts Tongue - Phyllitis scolopendrium

Polypody - Polypodium vulgare

Hard Shield fern - P. aculeatum

Soft Shield fern   - P. setiferum

Lemon Scented fern - Thelypteris oreopteris

Specialities of woods in the Chilterns

Coral-root (Cardamine bulbifera)

Lesser Wintergreen (Pyrola minor)

Yellow Birds nest (Monotropa)

Mezereon (Daphne mezereon)

Ghost orchid (Epipogium aphyllum)

Narrow lipped helleborine (E.leptochila)

Green flower helleborine (E. phyllanthes)

Chilterns Ancient Woodland Survey

Wood: _____ Grid Ref: _____ Date of Visit: _____

Damage	Occurrence	Comments
Invasive species	Yes / No	
Rubbish, rubble, garden waste	Yes / No	
Livestock / deer damage	Yes / No	
Garden extension/landscaping	Yes / No	
Clearance /earthworks	Yes / No	
Recreation	Yes / No	
Invasive Species		
Rhododendron	Yes / No	
Cherry laurel	Yes / No	
Himalayan balsam	Yes / No	
Sycamore	Yes / No	
Japanese knotweed	Yes / No	
Bamboo / other	Yes / No	
Uses		
Garden extension	Yes / No	
Recreation (inc equestrian)	Yes / No	
Game keeping	Yes / No	
Livestock	Yes / No	
Nature reserve	Yes / No	
Management		
Unmanaged coppice /standards	Yes / No	
Recent managed planting /felling	Yes / No	
Part or all conifer plantation	Yes / No	
Pollards / veteran trees	Yes / No	
High forest (beech/ oak)	Yes / No	
Boundary features		
Stream or ditch	Yes / No	
Remnants of bank, ditch &hedge	Yes / No	
Pollards, stubs, standards	Yes / No	
Remnants of bank & hedge	Yes / No	
Remnants of outgrown hedge	Yes / No	
Internal Archaeology		
Iron slag	Yes / No	
Pits - ponds	Yes / No	
Pits - quarries	Yes / No	
Pits - sawpits	Yes / No	
Pits - charcoal	Yes / No	
Pits - other	Yes / No	
Bank/ ditch – internal	Yes / No	
Drainage ditch	Yes / No	
Other – built structure	Yes / No	
Lynchets	Yes / No	
Sunken trackways	Yes / No	
Other	Yes / No	
Habitat		
Comments		